FREE TRADE AND FRUSTRATION

KARL F. HELLEINER

Free Trade and Frustration: Anglo-Austrian Negotiations 1860-70

UNIVERSITY OF TORONTO PRESS

© University of Toronto Press 1973
Toronto and Buffalo
Printed in Canada
ISBN 0-8020-1895-5
Microfiche ISBN 0-8020-0236-6
LC 72-80645

Contents

Preface

The involved negotiations between Austria and Great Britain which led to the signing of two commercial treaties in the 1860s have been made the subject of historical research before. Chapters IX and XI of Adolf Beer's *Die österreichische Handelspolitik im neunzehnten Jahrhundert* (Vienna, 1891) contain a succinct account of those diplomatic moves. But Beer's narrative was based exclusively on documents preserved in the Austrian State archives. The present study, by drawing also on the rich documentary evidence available in the Public Record Office (London) will, it is hoped, broaden, and to some extent modify, Beer's account of an episode in commercial diplomacy that sheds light on Britain's patient endeavour to convert other nations to a policy of Free Trade, as well as on the dogged resistance which these efforts encountered from continental businessmen and bureaucrats.

I am greatly indebted to the Canada Council and my university for generous grants which enabled me to undertake this study. Grateful recognition is also due to the staffs of the Public Record Office(London), the Haus-, Hof-und Staatsarchiv (Vienna), the Finanz-und Hofkammerarchiv (Vienna), and the Nationalbibliothek (Vienna) for their hospitality and assistance in obtaining xerox copies of unpublished documents. Requests for other photographic prints were kindly met by Miss P.J. Willets, Assistant Keeper in the Manuscript Department of the British Museum, by the Keeper of the Bodleian Library, and by Dr Michael Stickler, Director of the Austrian Parliamentary Library. Unpublished Crown-copyright material in the Public Record Office has been reproduced by permission of the Controller of HM Stationery Office. My friends Dr Albert E.J. Hollaender, Dr Richard Blaas, Director of the Haus-, Hof-und and Staatsarchiv, and Dr Alfred Hoffmann, Professor of Economic History in the University of Vienna, have obliged me by readily answering various inquiries. Miss Hazel Neary and Mrs Hoare, Assistant Keepers in the Public Record Office, have rendered assistance in the selection of documents for reproduction.

I wish to record my special gratitude to my colleagues V.W. Bladen, Richard Gregor, Samuel Hollander, John H.A. Munro, and A.M. Watson, who, after reading the whole or sizeable portions of my typescript, revived my flagging energy by encouraging comments.

K.F.H.
University of Toronto
June 1972

FREE TRADE AND FRUSTRATION

ABBREVIATIONS

PRO Public Record Office, London
HHStA Haus-, Hof- und Staatsarchiv, Vienna
FHKA Finanz- und Hofkammerarchiv, Vienna
AVA Allgemeines Verwaltungsarchiv, Vienna

Introduction

The protracted negotiations which resulted in the conclusion of a commercial treaty between Austria and Britain in 1865, the signing of a supplementary convention in 1868, and the revision of these earlier agreements under the terms of yet another treaty at the end of 1869 do not compare in dramatic intensity with the sequence of proposals and decisions which, in the short space of three months, had a few years previously led to the signature of a similar instrument – the Cobden-Chevalier treaty of 1860. Nor, in the case of Austria, was the eventual break with the inherited principles of prohibition and high protection as decisive as were the changes in the commercial policy of France to which the government of Napoleon III had assented under that treaty. For the rest, the partial dismantling of the Austrian tariff wall was not nearly as important to British trade as was the opening up of the French market. As William Gladstone put it in his Financial Statement of 1865, a reduction of the Austrian tariff was not 'a matter of vital or even of sensible importance to England.'[1] Still, a move, however tardy and reluctant, on the part of yet another Great Power toward economic liberalism was not without significance: it promised to reinforce what many contemporaries regarded as an irreversible trend towards free exchanges

1 W.E. Gladstone, *The Financial Statements of 1853 and 1860 to 1865* (London, 1865), 1865 statement, p. 25.

and international division of labour, a development which, it was hoped, would conduce to worldwide economic growth and amity among nations.

However it is not only the outcome but also the progress of those Anglo-Austrian negotiations that is of interest to the historian. For their story sheds new light on the missionary zeal with which British businessmen and diplomats preached the glad tidings of Free Trade to the children of Protectionist darkness: it illustrates as well the powerful resistance which the new faith encountered whenever more than lip service was demanded of reluctant converts. A study of those negotiations, moreover, clearly reveals how purely political considerations – the turns and twists of Austria's domestic policies no less than the exigencies of her foreign relations – influenced and at times determined their course.

Paradoxically it was experiments with parliamentary institutions that created the most serious obstacles for a policy of economic liberalism in Austria. The change, after the military disasters of 1859 and 1866, from a neo-absolutist regime to one that accorded the bourgeoisie an – albeit limited – voice in public affairs meant that the government of Francis Joseph had to pay heed to the wishes of that newly enfranchised class, a class whose members, almost to a man, believed in Protection. But even before the newly convoked *Reichsrat* provided a parliamentary forum for the spokesmen of the manufacturing interest the cause of Protection in Austria had found influential champions among the high bureaucracy, especially in the Ministry of Commerce. Its dogged resistance to liberal tariff reforms on more than one occasion thwarted diplomatic designs of Foreign Ministers who, for reasons connected with Austria's German ambitions or in an attempt to obtain Britain's political support, were inclined towards a policy of economic liberalism.

The British Cabinet and its representatives in Vienna, aware of the powerful forces that were opposed to the tariff changes which they asked Austria to enact, showed remarkable patience with the fitful course of the negotiation. Though the repeated protestations of liberal intentions to which they were treated by successive Austrian Ministers can hardly have carried much con-

viction, since they were invariably followed by evasions, tergiver-
sations, and pathetic subterfuges, the British put their trust in
the eventual triumph of economic logic and the persuasive power
of commercial statistics. They could appeal to the happy experience of the French with the policy of economic liberalism which
the Cobden treaty had initiated. 'In the commercial relations
between Great Britain and France,' William Hutt, the Vice-
President of the Board of Trade, told the Austrians in 1865,

up to the year 1860, we have a striking illustration of the pernicious
operation of [a policy of high Protection]; and what is fortunate, we
have ever since that period the happy results of the opposite. The working
of the two systems is thus brought in presence of each other, and the
contrast is complete. Previous to 1860, that is previous to the memorable
treaty between France and England, notwithstanding the free access
which France enjoyed to the English market, the commercial intercourse
between these neighbouring countries was insignificant and almost station-
ary. In 1860 France revised her tariff, and an instantaneous change
took place in her trade with England. That trade is now more than
double of what it was then, and is by far the most important trade which
France carries on with any State in Europe.[2]

The British were convinced that a liberal reform of the Austrian
tariff, such as the proposed treaty of commerce with them would
provide for, was of 'incalculable and urgent importance to Austria,'
and 'would impart a new impulse to the productive forces of
the Empire.'[3] Louis Mallet, who was the chief British negotiator
in 1867, was undoubtedly sincere when he assured the Austrian
Minister of Foreign Affairs that

the tenacity of purpose which Her Majesty's government had displayed
throughout these protracted negotiations arose, not, as was supposed
by the Austrian Protectionists, from any expectation of obtaining for

2 A memorandum drawn up by Hutt and read by Robert B.D. Morier at the
  inaugural meeting of the joint Anglo-Austrian Commission of Inquiry on 22
  April 1865; enclosed in Hutt's dispatch to Earl Russell of 27 April 1865: PRO,
  FO 425/79.
3 Mallet's dispatch to Lord Stanley of 20 May 1867: PRO, FO 425/90.

British trade, at all events for some time to come, great or special advantages, but from their anxious wish to carry on the great international policy commenced by the Anglo-French treaty in 1860, and in this view to bring into the great current of commercial progress an Empire possessing resources which, when freely developed, must add immeasurably to the wealth, and raise the standard of well-being in all the countries of Europe.[4]

But while emphasizing their country's unselfish motives the British negotiators could not leave the Austrians in doubt that any agreement with them would have to satisfy 'the numerous and important interests in the United Kingdom which are more or less affected by the conditions of our export trade';[5] and they freely admitted that their government had to insist on 'the attainment of solid and practical commercial advantages in the general results of any arrangement which might be made.'[6] Though the almost tabooed word 'reciprocity' was carefully avoided, this smacked of economic heresy. To demand 'solid and practical commercial advantages' was inconsistent with the abstract doctrine of Free Trade. Even Gladstone, whose ideology was tempered with political realism, had on an earlier occasion admitted that 'a commercial treaty would be an abandonment of the principles of Free Trade, ... if it were founded on what I may call haggling exchanges.'[7] But how was it possible to negotiate a treaty of commerce without at least a modicum of 'haggling'?

Free Trade doctrinarians would reply that it was unnecessary to conclude commercial agreements. Their notion found ultimate expression in the maxim 'Take care of your imports, and your exports will take care of themselves.' But a policy of inaction suggested by a school of thought which, to use Louis Mallet's words, 'strenuously denounced and resisted all attempts to secure the cooperation of foreign countries in establishing reciprocity of freedom, as if it were only less objectionable than reciprocity

4 Ibid.
5 Mallet's dispatch to Lord Stanley of 25 June 1867: ibid.
6 Mallet's dispatch to Lord Stanley of 11 July 1867: ibid.
7 Gladstone, *Financial Statements*, 1860 statement, p. 136.

in monopoly,'[8] did not appeal to the British government and their advisers. Though they knew very well that their bargaining power was weak – Britain having unilaterally renounced almost all protective devices – they were not averse to engaging in wide-ranging commercial diplomacy. As a matter of fact the Austrian treaty of commerce was only one of eight major conventions of this type negotiated and concluded by Britain during the 1860s.[9]

This is a study in commercial diplomacy, not an exercise in the theory of international trade. Attention will be focused on men's actions and their motives rather than on the logical soundness of their economic reasoning or the validity and mutual consistency of their basic assumptions. This is not to deny that commercial policies were influenced by the economic creed of the decision-makers – be it an unqualified faith in the blessings of Free Trade or the firmly held conviction that the development of a relatively backward economy requires a policy of Protection. But the impact of such beliefs on people's actions is a function of the strength with which those convictions are held (which may themselves be related to individual or group interests), not of their intrinsic validity. Thus for the historian of commercial diplomacy there is no need to demonstrate the limitations of doctrinaire Free Trade or to expose the fallacies of crude Protectionism.

8 Sir Louis Mallet. *Reciprocity: a Letter to Mr. Thomas Bayley Potter, M.P.*, printed for the Cobden Club (London. Paris & New York. [1879]), pp. 14f.
9 Sir John Clapham, *An Economic History of Modern Britain*, vol. II (Cambridge, 1932), p. 247.

1
The diplomacy of rags

When Gladstone in his financial statement of 1860 announced to the House of Commons his intention to abolish, together with the excise, the customs duties on paper,[1] he was aware that this measure would call forth vigorous protests from a mildly ailing industry. It was generally known that the British papermakers, like those of other countries, were faced with a chronic scarcity of their most important raw material, rags.[2] The imposition by a number of European countries of export prohibitions or stiff export duties on rags had long since caused English supplies from continental sources to diminish and prices to rise. More recently the decision of the Austrian government to double the duty on exports of rags from Trieste had provided a glaring example of this protectionist policy.[3]

1 W.E. Gladstone, *The Financial Statements of 1853 and 1860 to 1865* (London, 1865), pp. 158 and 174.
2 D.C. Coleman, *The British Paper Industry 1495–1860* (Oxford, 1958), pp. 337f.
3 This matter became the subject of lengthy correspondence between Lord Augustus Loftus, the British Ambassador to the Court of Vienna, and the Foreign Office in 1860. See, e.g., Loftus's dispatch to Lord John Russell of 12 April 1860 with enclosure (the copy of a report submitted to him by Charles Thomas Hill, the British Vice-Consul at Fiume): PRO, FO 7/592; draft of a Foreign Office instruction for Loftus of 9 May 1860: PRO, FO 7/587; Loftus's dispatch of 19 July 1860 with enclosures (a copy of his note addressed to Count Rechberg, the Austrian Minister of Foreign Affairs, and the report of a commission set up by the Chamber of Commerce of Lower Austria, voicing opposition to an abolition of the export duty on rags): PRO, FO 7/595.

Arguments based on the fact that their foreign competitors enjoyed an advantage in the shape of those export duties and prohibitions had once before, in 1853, enabled the British paper-makers to avert too drastic a reduction of the customs duties on paper imports.[4] It was only to be expected that they and their spokesmen in Parliament would once again put up a strenuous opposition to a policy that might expose the industry to some gentle breezes of foreign competition. As it was, the second reading of the Paper Duty Repeal Bill was carried by a majority of 53 in the House of Commons.[5] But opposition was growing: at the third reading, on 8 May 1860, the majority of the government was reduced to 9, and two weeks later the bill was thrown out in the House of Lords by a majority of 89.[6] Some kind of compromise was reached in August, but it was only in June of the following year that Gladstone had his way: his Financial Bill for 1861–2, which once again provided for the repeal of the customs duties on paper, was passed by both Houses of Parliament.[7]

Meanwhile the government, with a view to taking the wind out of the papermakers' sail, was making determined efforts to persuade the Austrian authorities to abolish, or at least reduce, their very high duty on the exportation of rags.[8] (France, under a recently concluded commercial treaty – the so-called Cobden Treaty – had already agreed to lift her prohibition of exports of rags, and replace it by a duty of £4 17s 2d per ton.[9]) The conjuncture seemed not inauspicious for such an attempt. In pursuance of her policy of economic liberalism Britain had extended to all other nations the tariff concessions which she had recently

4 Coleman, pp. 326f.
5 Sir Stafford H. Northcote, *Twenty Years of Financial Policy* (London, 1862), p. 356.
6 Ibid.
7 Coleman, p. 331.
8 The obvious connection between Gladstone's policy of repeal and those diplomatic efforts was commented upon by Carl Freiherr von Godrich in a letter of 22 July 1860 to Count Apponyi, the Austrian Ambassador to the Court of St James, which the latter enclosed in his dispatch of 25 July 1860 to Count Rechberg, the Austrian Minister of Foreign Affairs: HHStA, Politisches Archiv VIII, England, Karton 53.
9 Coleman, p. 331, n. 2.

granted to the French under the Cobden Treaty.[10] As far as Austria was concerned, the reduction of British duties on foreign wines – an immediate one which was to be followed, after 1 April 1861, by a drastic lowering of the rates on light wines[11] – was of particular importance: it gave promise of opening the British market to Austrian and more especially Hungarian wines. Not surprisingly, the British move 'produced a very favourable impression' upon the Austrian authorities.[12] Was it too much to hope that the Imperial government could be induced to reciprocate? On 18 April 1860 Britain's Ambassador to the Court of Vienna, Lord Augustus Loftus, was instructed by the Foreign Office to try. He was to point to the happy experiences which Britain had had with her policy of Free Trade, and 'express the earnest hope of Her Majesty's government that the Austrian government may by a reduction of duties on British produce and manufactures ... promote the commerce between the two countries, which is at present far less than it might be under a freer system.'[13] Count Rechberg, the Austrian Premier and Minister of Foreign Affairs, seems to have interpreted Loftus's representations as an invitation on the part of the British government to conclude a treaty of commerce;[14] but he may have read too much into the Ambassador's words – unless Loftus had used more specific language than his instruction warranted. For the time being at any rate the Foreign Office does not seem to have envisaged negotiations leading to a convention. A subsequent instruction of 9 May 1860 merely directed Loftus to draw Rechberg's attention to the exorbitant increase in the Austrian export duty on rags, which had caused shipments of this commodity from Trieste to cease altogether. 'Such a state of things is as injurious to the commercial and fiscal interests

10 Gladstone, p. 133.
11 Ibid.
12 Loftus's dispatch of 26 January 1860: PRO, FO 7/589.
13 Instruction for Loftus (draft) of 18 April 1860: PRO, FO 7/586.
14 In a dispatch to Count Apponyi of 1 May 1860 Rechberg reported as follows:
   'Aussi est-ce avec une grande satisfaction que j'ai entendu Lord A. Loftus me dire, la dernière fois qu'il a été chez moi, qu'il avait à me communiquer des propositions de son gouvernement relativement à un traité de commerce.'
   HHStA, Politisches Archiv VIII, England, Karton 54.

of Austria herself as it must be damaging to the trade which foreign countries might be willing to enter into with Austrian ports.'[15]

Count Rechberg appears to have listened to this appeal in a receptive spirit. He 'expressed his anxious wish to do all in his power to remove any restrictions which had hitherto retarded the greater development of the commerce of Austria with foreign States'; and he asked Loftus 'to address a note to him on the subject, as it would enable him to bring the subject more easily before the Finance Department, which is now charged with the direction of all commercial affairs.'[16] The Ambassador was slow in complying with this request. His formal note – a long homily on the blessings of Free Trade, supported by statistical data – was not handed in before 10 July 1860;[17] nor did it contain any proposal to negotiate a commercial agreement.

London's reserve was all the more puzzling since the general climate of Anglo-Austrian relations, which for some time past had been exceedingly chilly, had lately given promise of improvement. Alarmed by Napoleon's annexation of Nice and Savoy and apprehensive of even more ambitious designs on the part of the French Emperor, the directors of Britain's foreign policy seemed inclined to pay more attention to Austria.[18] As Count Rechberg reported to his ministerial colleagues on 23 June 1860, Lord Palmerston had let him know through a confidential agent that his government was prepared to establish closer political relations with Austria, provided Vienna took the initiative by reducing the export duties on ship's timber and rags.[19]

Rechberg, whatever his views on the intrinsic merits of Free

---

15 Instruction for Loftus (draft) of 9 May 1860: PRO, FO 7/587.
16 Loftus's dispatch of 16 May 1860: PRO, FO 7/593.
17 Loftus enclosed a copy of this note in his dispatch of 19 July 1860: PRO, FO 7/595.
18 Herbert C.F. Bell, *Lord Palmerston* (London, 1936), II, 247ff.
19 HHStA, Kabinettsarchiv, Ministerratsprotokolle, 23 June 1860, The name of the agent – Defcher – is mentioned repeatedly in the Rechberg-Apponyi correspondence. That it was he who transmitted Palmerston's proposal is stated in Rechberg's letter to Apponyi (draft) of 1 July 1860: HHStA, Politisches Archiv VIII, England, Karton 54.

Trade, could only welcome these overtures. His country, having lately been led into dangerous isolation by its singularly inept foreign policy, had suffered a humiliating defeat the previous year at the hands of the French and the Piedmontese, and now stood in dire need of diplomatic support, if only to restrain the Court of Turin from further aggression. Of this necessity Count Rechberg in his capacity as Minister of Foreign Affairs was keenly aware; and he knew that under the circumstances Britain was the only one among the Great Powers with which a *rapprochement* was conceivable. His trend of thought is revealed in a private letter to Count Apponyi, the Austrian Ambassador in London, in which he declared himself strongly in favour of closer trading relations with Britain: they would give Austria 'not only commercial but also political advantages.'[20]

Palmerston's tentative offer was discussed at some length in two meetings of the Austrian Council of Ministers.[21] As was to be expected the proposed reduction of the export duty on timber and more especially of that on rags – the latter amounted to 2 Florins per cwt on exports by sea and 4 Florins on exports across land frontiers – was strenuously opposed by the spokesman of the German bourgeoisie in Austria, Ignaz von Plener, the acting Minister of Finance. He freely admitted that a lowering of these duties would not entail any substantial sacrifice of revenue, and might indeed be advantageous from a fiscal point of view. But he reminded his colleagues that the government had only recently given the Austrian industrialists a formal undertaking[22] not to introduce any changes in the tariff before 1865, except as a consequence of a commercial treaty with a foreign State. An Anglo-Austrian convention, however, would be of no economic advantage, since Britain had already gone so far in the reduction or

---

20 Rechberg to Apponyi (draft), 14 February 1860: HHStA, Politisches Archiv VIII, England, Karton 54 (trans.).
21 HHStA, Kabinettsarchiv, Ministerratsprotokolle, 26 June and 30 June 1860.
22 The reference is to an Imperial Decree of 20 December 1859. See the newspaper clipping enclosed in Loftus's dispatch of 19 July 1860: PRO, FO 7/595 and the minutes of the Austrian Council of Ministers of 30 June 1860: HHStA, Kabinettsarchiv, Ministerratsprotokolle.

abolition of her customs duties that she had nothing to offer to foreign countries.[23] As for possible benefits of a political nature, these, von Plener argued, could hardly be stipulated in a treaty of commerce. For the rest, the requested reduction of the export duty on rags would certainly cause the Austrian papermakers to renew their clamour, which had only recently been allayed by an upward revision of that duty.

Von Plener's objections were brushed aside by Count Rechberg. Insisting on the primacy of politics he declared that to gain Britain's goodwill – the minutes of the Council of Ministers used the word 'alliance' – was a matter of such importance under the circumstances that minor considerations had to be overruled. He therefore asked for authorization to start immediate negotiations with Lord Augustus Loftus. After some debate Rechberg's view that Austria could not afford to reject the British overtures was accepted by a majority of the Ministers.

Having received the backing of his Cabinet Count Rechberg lost no time informing both Count Apponyi[24] and the British Ambassador[25] of his desire to start formal negotiations with Britain. 'In the matter of tariff concessions,' the Premier promised, 'we shall not show ourselves unyielding, since we do not lose sight of the great object of complete understanding in the political field.'[26] Such concessions, however, would have to be embodied in a treaty of commerce because of the recent promise by the Emperor (see above, p. 12, n. 22) not to make any changes in the existing tariff for a period of five years. (The government of Napoleon III, who had given the French manufacturers a similar promise, had recently used the same expedient – recourse to

---

23 This point had already been urged by Count Apponyi in a private letter to Rechberg of 1 March 1860 (HHStA, Politisches Archiv VIII, England, Karton 54) and by the Austrian Ministry of Finance in a note to Rechberg of 14 March 1860 (FHKA, Präsidium FM, G.Z. 778/1860).

24 Rechberg to Apponyi (draft), 1 July 1860: HHStA, Politisches Archiv VIII, England, Karton 54.

25 Loftus's dispatch of 5 July 1860: PRO, FO 7/595.

26 Rechberg to Apponyi, 1 July 1860: HHStA, Politisches Archiv VIII, England, Karton 54 (trans.).

the treaty-making powers of the sovereign – to effect a liberalization of the French tariff.[27])

In his conversations with Lord Augustus Loftus Rechberg
expressed a wish that the negotiations should be carried on in
Vienna. He gave as his reason 'that a pressure might be required
here to overcome local scruples and difficulties, which he could
usefully exercise if the seat of negotiation were at Vienna, but
which it would be very difficult for him to do if the negotiations
were carried on in London.'[28] Rechberg obviously was anxious
to make the British statesmen appreciate these difficulties – 'a
very strong protectionist feeling both in the official regions and
in the manufacturing classes'[29] – and he asked Count Apponyi
to plead with them for understanding. Defending a policy of
economic liberalism before the newly created *Reichsrat*, a parliamentary body in which the protectionists were strongly represented, would be no easy task for the Austrian government.[30]

If Rechberg had counted on Britain's eager acceptance of
his proposal to start commercial negotiations forthwith he was
to be disappointed. Lord Palmerston at any rate did not seem
to be in a hurry. In his dispatch of 11 July 1860 the Prime Minister
instructed Loftus to communicate to the Austrian government
his willingness to enter into negotiations, but added that it would
be convenient 'to wait for a period of three months in order
to see what will be the ultimate tariff of specific duties to be
fixed by the treaty between this country and France, and also
to ascertain how far the Protectionists of Austria may be disposed
to bend their selfish interests and obstinate prejudices for the
benefit of Austria.'[31]

Palmerston could hardly expect the Austrian Protectionists to
undergo a conversion between July and October. The real reason

27 See Arthur L. Dunham, *The Anglo-French Treaty of Commerce of 1860 and
   the Progress of the Industrial Revolution in France* (Ann Arbor, 1930), pp.
   98 and 131.
28 Loftus's dispatch of 5 July 1860: PRO, FO 7/595.
29 Ibid.
30 Rechberg to Apponyi, 1 July 1860: HHStA, Politisches Archiv VIII, England,
   Karton 54.
31 Palmerston's instruction for Loftus (draft) of 11 July 1860: PRO, FO 7/587.

why he refused to enter into negotiations at that moment was of course a different one. As Count Apponyi observed in one of his reports from London,[32] the Prime Minister, never an ardent friend of the Habsburg monarchy, was having second thoughts about an Anglo-Austrian *entente*.[33] Under his leadership the British Cabinet, just like other governments, was apt to subordinate its commercial policies to the changing exigencies of foreign affairs. As a spokesman for England's mercantile interest complained: 'Whereas we, simple men of business, have nothing in view whatever except to trade as much as we can with every nation under Heaven, a treaty of commerce in the hands of an English Minister becomes a piece with which to play on the chessboard of Europe. If there happens to be a disposition on the part of the English Minister to go against Austria, he will throw cold water and discourage a commercial treaty; but if, on the other hand, for political reasons he sees fit to back Austria, then we may expect he will support a commercial treaty.'[34]

Count Rechberg, however, does not seem to have been seriously disturbed by Palmerston's vacillation. He stubbornly pursued his object of a political *rapprochement* with Britain, whose goodwill he still hoped to purchase with commercial concessions. On 5 October 1860 he informed the British Chargé d'Affaires[35] that the Imperial government were now prepared, in fulfilment of London's wishes, to lower the rates of duty levied upon rags exported from the Austrian dominions. In view of the Emperor's

---

32 The dispatch in question does not seem to be extant; but its contents are summed up in a memorandum of 27 August 1860, drawn up by Baron Hock, a high-ranking official in the Austrian Ministry of Finance: FHKA, Präsidium FM, G.Z. 3211/1860.

33 Indeed Palmerston may not have been very serious about the whole business to start with: otherwise he would almost certainly have transmitted his proposals through ordinary diplomatic channels rather than through a private emissary.

34 Mr Crawshay in a speech before the Newcastle Chamber of Commerce, as reported in the *Northern Daily Express*, 4 November 1862: HHStA, Administrative Registratur, F34, Handel, Grossbritannien, Karton 5. (Newspaper clipping sent to Rechberg by the Austrian Consul General in London.) I have changed the wording from oblique to direct oration.

35 Julian Fane's dispatch to the Foreign Office of 5 October 1860: FO 7/598.

engagement not to make any changes in the tariff it would be necessary, however, to give this unilateral concession the form of a commercial convention. Rechberg proposed that such an instrument should consist of a single article, embodying a declaration that in return for the benefits likely to accrue to Austrian commerce from the operation of the recent commercial treaty between Great Britain and France, the stipulations of which extended to all nations, the Austrian government engaged to diminish the existing duties upon rags exported from the Imperial dominions.'[36] On the day after his interview with the British Chargé d'Affaires Count Rechberg apprised the Council of Ministers of his diplomatic initiative,[37] and obtained the grudging assent of the acting Minister of Finance, who on this occasion reported on encouraging results of recent experiments, undertaken by the Austrian State Printing Office, which seemed to show that maize straw could successfully be substituted for rags in the manufacture of paper.[38]

London's response to Rechberg's offer was once again curiously evasive. Loftus was instructed to tell Count Rechberg that his government welcomed the intended reduction of the export duty on rags, but were 'inclined to think that it should be embodied in the general treaty of commerce of which Her Majesty's government will very shortly propose a draft.'[39] No such *projet*, however, was submitted by the British; instead, nine months later London decided to take up Rechberg's proposal of a *brief* convention after all. On 31 July 1861 Lord Bloomfield, who in the meantime had replaced Lord Augustus Loftus as Ambassador to the Court of Vienna, received instructions to offer Austria a treaty which, in return for a reduction of the export duty on rags, would contain a British undertaking not to impose a differential duty on Austrian paper imported into the United Kingdom.[40]

36 Ibid.
37 HHStA, Kabinettsarchiv, Ministerratsprotokolle, 6 October 1860.
38 Ibid.
39 Instruction for Loftus (draft) of 31 October 1860: PRO, FO 7/588.
40 Instruction for Bloomfield (draft) of 31 July 1861: PRO, FO 7/605; Bloomfield's note to Rechberg (copy) of 6 August 1861: PRO, FO 7/612.

The British demand did not go beyond what Rechberg himself had offered the previous autumn; but it became apparent at once that it now had little chance of being accepted by the Austrian government. In his conversations with Bloomfield Count Rechberg repeated what he had hinted at on an earlier occasion[41]: that Britain had missed her opportunity when she failed to enter into the agreement he had proposed the previous October. The constitutional changes which had recently come into force in Austria required that commercial treaties be submitted to the *Reichsrat*, whose protectionist majority was certain to disapprove of unilateral tariff concessions.[42] Rechberg added, however, that opposition might be overcome if Britain were 'to introduce into the proposed convention an article that would insure to trade between Austria and England the advantages conceded to France by [the] late treaty, or those enjoyed by the most favoured nations, or something in fact that would have the appearance of a *concession* to Austria.'[43]

Not surprisingly London categorically rejected these far-reaching demands. Bloomfield was directed[44] to notify the Imperial government in writing that 'Her Majesty's government could not, in return for the modification of the Austrian export duty upon one article of comparatively small commercial importance, consent to extend *by treaty* to Austria either the advantages recently conferred upon French trade in return for large concessions, or the advantages possessed by the most favoured nation, unless a corrresponding stipulation were made on the part of Austria. Her Majesty's government think that the stipulation already proposed by them respecting the non-imposition of duty on the importation of Austrian paper is a proper equivalent for the contemplated reduction of the Austrian duty on the export of rags.'[45]

41 Bloomfield's dispatch of 20 June 1861: PRO, FO 7/611.
42 Bloomfield's dispatch of 22 August 1861: PRO, FO 7/613.
43 Ibid.
44 Instruction for Bloomfield (draft) of 23 September 1861: PRO, FO 7/605.
45 Ibid., italics mine. See also Bloomfield's note to Rechberg (copy) of 3 October 1861: PRO, FO 7/614.

The Austrian government could not fail to realize that London's conditional offer not to introduce a differential customs duty on Austrian paper imports was meant as a warning. What they could not be sure of was whether the British, in case of an Austrian refusal, would make good their implied threat. It was with a view to obtaining some indication of London's intentions that Rechberg directed Count Wimpffen, the Austrian Chargé d'Affaires in London, to report on the following[46]: Has the British government explicitly reserved to themselves the power of introducing differential duties against nations which fail to grant to England hoped-for tariff reductions in return for the advantages accruing to them in consequence of the Anglo-French treaty of commerce? And if so, has this power been used? Wimpffen's dispatch of 17 October 1861[47] reassured Count Rechberg on both these points: the Act by which the paper duties had recently been repealed (24 Vic. c. xx) did not provide for any exceptions; nor was it possible to instance a single case of an imposition of differential duties.

Wimpffen's encouraging reply was based on a memorandum whose author, Ritter von Schaeffer, the Director of the Austrian consulate in London, had found it necessary, however, to add a caveat. 'The English government,' he wrote, 'must after all know best what their powers are, and whether they can obtain the subsequent sanction of Parliament for regulations that would deprive other nations of the advantages flowing from the Anglo-French treaty of commerce, if they refuse to offer a quid pro quo.'[48] In this context Herr von Schaeffer also referred to a growing sense of irritation among British industrialists, who resented Gladstone's policy of sweeping and unrequited tariff reductions, and he predicted that foreign governments would find it advisable, on grounds of equity and for political reasons, to offer Britain reciprocal concessions.

Count Rechberg, for one, did not need to be reminded of the

46 Instruction for Wimpffen (draft) of 9 October 1861: HHStA, Administrative Registratur, F34, Handel, Grossbritannien, Karton 5.
47 Ibid.
48 Von Schaeffer's letter to Count Wimpffen of 15 October 1861: HHStA, Administrative Registratur, F34, Handel, Grossbritannien, Karton 5 (trans.).

linkages between economic and political matters; but von Schaeffer's memorandum seems to have confirmed him in his view that Austria could no longer afford to prevaricate. He therefore decided to resume his efforts to obtain from his ministerial colleagues approval of a policy of accommodation. In a lengthy note addressed to the Minister of Trade, Count Wickenburg,[49] Rechberg emphasized that it would not do to antagonize British public opinion and Palmerston's Cabinet by refusing to treat or by raising inordinate demands without offering much in return. Rather than insist that Britain bind herself by treaty to grant Austria most-favoured-nation status as a quid pro quo for a reduction of her export duty on rags, the Imperial government should be prepared to conclude a convention containing a *mutual* most-favoured-nation clause. All in all Rechberg left no doubt that he was anxious to act upon the suggestions advanced by Lord Bloomfield in his note of 3 October.

Notwithstanding Count Rechberg's pressing request for a speedy reply, his note to Wickenburg remained unanswered. Thus, when in March 1862 Lord Bloomfield (who had been instructed by the Foreign Office to sound Wickenburg out about a visit to Vienna of one of Britain's chief commercial negotiators)[50] inquired about the prospects of an Anglo-Austrian accord, Rechberg could not but be non-committal.[51] The whole business seemed to have reached a dead end. Soon afterwards, however, events supervened that introduced a new element into the commercial policy of Austria, and forced her statesmen to reconsider the possibility of coming to terms with Britain.

49 Rechberg to Wickenburg, 24 October 1861 (draft): ibid.
50 Instruction for Bloomfield (draft) of 12 March 1862: PRO, FO 7/625.
51 Bloomfield's dispatch of 13 March 1862: PRO, FO 7/629.

2
A missionary effort

In their bitter struggle for hegemony in Germany both Austria and Prussia had had recourse to the weapons of economic diplomacy and warfare long before they sought a military decision on the battlefield of Sadowa.[1] As far as the Habsburg monarchy was concerned, one of its avowed aims ever since 1849 had been to gain admission to the German Customs Union, with a view to assuming the leadership of the protectionist minority in the Union. Prussia, however, by manoeuvres that were on occasion as ruthless as they were skilful, had succeeded in warding off this challenge to her ascendancy. In the end Vienna had had to content herself with a commercial treaty with Prussia, signed on 19 February 1853, which, while it provided for some mutual tariff concessions, held out only vague prospects of Austria's admission to the *Zollverein* by 1865.

Even this remote and uncertain chance, however, seemed to be slipping away when, in the spring of 1862, it became known that Prussia, making light of Austrian objections, was about to

---

1 The foregoing account of Prusso-Austrian relations is based very largely on Adolf Beer's well documented monograph *Die österreichische Handelspolitik im neunzehnten Jahrhundert* (Vienna, 1891) and on Karl Heinz Werner's chapter 'Österreichs Industrie- und Aussenhandelspolitik 1848 bis 1948,' in Hans Mayer, ed., *Hundert Jahre österreichischer Wirtschaftsentwicklung* (Vienna, 1949).

conclude a commercial treaty with France. If acceded to by the other governments of the *Zollverein* States this convention, by guaranteeing both parties most-favoured-nation treatment, would not only nullify the customs preferences to which Austria was entitled in her trade with members of the Union: by stipulating for very substantial reductions of the Prussian (and by implication of the Union) duties the proposed treaty would widen the existing gap between the high-protectionist tariff of Austria and that of the *Zollverein*, and thus effectively block the customs union with Germany so eagerly sought by the Habsburg monarchy.

Austria was determined to thwart what many of her statesmen believed to be an insidious Prussian design to prevent her from ever joining the German Customs Union. A last-minute attempt was to be made to induce other members of the *Zollverein* (and through them possibly even Prussia) to repudiate the French treaty in its present form. This strategy was not likely to succeed, however, unless Austria indicated that she was prepared to modify her policy of high Protection. A meeting of the Council of Ministers held on 24 April 1862 decided upon this course of action.[2]

Having been informed by Count Rechberg of this decision Lord Bloomfield lost no time reporting to London on what seemed to herald a decisive change in Austria's commercial policy.[3] He had been told by the Austrian Premier that in view of the Franco-Prussian treaty 'it had become the duty of the Imperial government seriously to consider the propriety of lowering the duties on importation into Austria ... and that it was now the settled opinion of the government that Austria must reduce her tariff with a view to place herself in the same advantageous position as other countries.' This was what London had been urging all along; and the Ambassador, obviously pleased, warmly congratulated Rechberg 'on the victory he had obtained.' But the latter found it necessary to caution him against too sanguine expectations: he replied 'that he most sincerely rejoiced in having been able to carry the question through the Cabinet, but that [Bloomfield] must still bear in mind that, although the Imperial government

2 HHStA, Kabinettsarchiv, Ministerratsprotokolle.
3 Bloomfield's dispatch of 1 May 1862: PRO, FO 7/631.

adopted the principle of Free Trade, the practical working out of this principle would be an affair of time.'

Though Rechberg's concluding remarks were calculated to dampen London's hopes, the British government decided at once to take advantage of the promised shift in Austria's general attitude. As early as 28 May 1862 Count Apponyi was able to pass on to his chief reliable information that the British Cabinet had recently given serious consideration to re-entering negotiations for a commercial convention with Austria.[4] As a matter of fact the Foreign Office two weeks later did transmit to Lord Bloomfield the draft of a treaty of commerce and navigation, with orders to communicate it to the Austrian government.[5] This document – a revised version of an earlier draft[6] that had been announced but never submitted to Vienna (see above, p. 16) – contained reciprocal most-favoured-nation clauses, as well as a stipulation that Austria should impose no higher duty than 15 per cent *ad valorem* on the importation of any article of British produce or manufacture, with a proviso that, if in any instance the duty was now lower than 15 per cent, it should not be raised during the continuance of the treaty (Article II). Duties imposed by Austria on exports to Britain and her dominions were not to exceed 5 per cent *ad valorem*, and if lower at present should not be increased (Article III).

These demands were clearly meant to be scaled down in the course of future negotiations. The British government could hardly expect Vienna to accept obligations that would go far beyond what the French had conceded in 1860. While under the Cobden Treaty[7] the maximum duty on enumerated British imports was set as high as 30 per cent (to be lowered to 25 per cent only after 1 October 1864), Austria was asked to limit her import duties on all British goods to a mere 15 per cent *ad valorem*. However Count Rechberg did not raise any serious objections

4 Apponyi's dispatch of 28 May 1862: HHStA, Politisches Archiv VIII, England, Karton 57.
5 Instruction for Bloomfield (draft) of 11 June 1862 with enclosure: PRO, FO 7/625.
6 Marginal note on a printed copy of the draft: PRO, FO 7/625.
7 Great Britain, Foreign Office, *British and Foreign State Papers* (1859–60), 13ff.

when presented with the British draft; rather he confined himself to a few general remarks, reiterating previous assurances of goodwill as well as the usual warning that his policy of economic liberalism would run into many difficulties. He cited the instance of the Austrian silk industry, which, he thought, would certainly require a protective duty higher than the proposed 15 per cent.[8]

Before Rechberg could formally deal with the British initiative on the diplomatic level he had to obtain the opinion of his colleagues in charge of the Ministries of Trade and Finance. In requesting their official comments on the proposed treaty[9] the Premier admitted that the uncertainties created by the pending Franco-Prussian convention might provide the Austrian government with an adequate excuse for not opening commercial negotiations at present. Yet, Rechberg argued, in view of the great importance of the British step a flat refusal to discuss the offer would be invidious, and might jeopardize the chances of a political *rapprochement*. For the time being, he suggested, no more was required than a preliminary reply, which need not take the form of specific counter-proposals, though it might indicate, in a general way, some of the points to which Austria must take exception.

Responding to Rechberg's request the Ministries of Trade and Finance each produced a lengthy memorandum.[10] They both thought that the present moment was inopportune for negotiating and concluding a commercial convention with Britain. For Austria to assume treaty obligations in tariff matters at this time, they argued, would be incompatible with her offer, recently submitted to the governments of the *Zollverein*, to join a general German

8 Bloomfield's dispatch of 19 June 1862: PRO, FO 7/632.
9 Rechberg's note to Count Wickenburg, the Minister of Trade (draft), of 24 June 1862: HHStA, Administrative Registratur, F34, Handel, Grossbritannien, Karton 5.
10 The note of the Ministry of Trade, dated 28 July 1862, was addressed to the Ministry of Finance, which transmitted it, together with its own memorandum of 27 August 1862, to Rechberg. A second note of the Ministry of Trade, dated 24 September 1862, was sent to Rechberg directly. The memoranda of 27 August and 24 September are to be found in HHStA, Administrative Registratur, F34, Handel, Grossbritannien, Karton 5. The first note of the Ministry of Trade is missing, but its contents can be inferred from the other two documents.

customs union and to adjust her tariff structure accordingly.[11]

But while the two Departments were in full agreement on this point they differed in their appraisal of the British draft. The Ministry of Finance explicitly dissociated itself from the wholly negative view taken by the Ministry of Trade, which declared the British demand of a maximum duty of 15 per cent *ad valorem* quite unacceptable. Though it conceded that it might be necessary for Austria to insist on a modification of the proposed system of *ad valorem* duties, and to stipulate for a higher maximum in the case of some commodities, the Ministry of Finance found the substance of the British proposals quite unexceptionable. Had not the Austrian government, in their recent offer to join a general German customs union, declared themselves ready to revise their policy of Protection? In any case Austria, 'engaged in a bold and bitter struggle with Prussia on the plane of commercial policy, must strive to win England for an ally,' and to convince her 'that we are in earnest about the liberal direction of our trade and tariff policies.'

It may seem surprising that a Department whose head, Ignaz von Plener, though a liberal in constitutional matters, had reservations about Free Trade, should on this occasion have given its qualified endorsement to a liberal line of economic policy. But then the authors of the memorandum left no doubt that they regarded their arguments as purely academic. Though Prussia, undeterred by Austria's counter-moves, had recently signed her commercial treaty with France (2 August 1862), Vienna was not prepared to abandon its efforts to gain admission to a German customs union; and as long as there remained even a faint hope of success the Austrian government could not possibly tie their hands in tariff matters. Even Count Rechberg had come to the conclusion that Anglo-Austrian negotiations would have to await the outcome of the German contest. 'The commercial future of Austria,' he told the British Chargé d'Affaires on 7 August

---

11 This refers to the Austrian circular note of 10 July 1862, whose contents were communicated to London by way of an Instruction sent to Count Apponyi (draft) on the same date: HHStA, Politisches Archiv VIII, England, Karton 59.

1862, 'depended so entirely upon the results of the proposal she had recently made to enter the *Zollverein* that, until those results were known, the Imperial government could not enter into negotiations of a commercial nature with Her Majesty's government. The proposed treaty must therefore for the moment remain in abeyance.'[12]

London, it seems, had not been too optimistic about the success of its initiative. Only a few days before Rechberg wrote *finis* to this chapter of Anglo-Austrian relations, Lord Palmerston, replying to a question in the House of Commons about the prospects of a commercial treaty with Austria, had warned against wishful thinking. 'Habits of protection in favour of native industry,' he said, '–however ill-founded the reasons may be – are very difficult to be eradicated ... Therefore people must not be over-sanguine as to any great change in Austrian commercial policy.'[13]

Recognition of the strength of Austrian Protectionism and Rechberg's rejection of their advances did not yet, however, cause the British government to abandon their efforts to get a negotiation with Austria started. To open up new markets for British products must have appeared all the more desirable at a moment when home trade was slack and Anglo-American intercourse disrupted by the War of Secession. A reception given by the city of Southampton on 27 October 1862 to Baron Adolph Thierry, a former Austrian Cabinet Minister,[14] provided Lord Palmerston with an opportunity to deliver a speech on the blessings of Free Trade, and to issue a warm plea for closer commercial relations between

12 Julian Fane's dispatch of 7 August 1862: PRO, FO 7/635.
13 *Parliamentary Debates* (Hansard), 3rd s., vol. CLXVIII, col. 1207 (4 August 1862). The question had been raised by Mr. Somerset A. Beaumont, Member for Newcastle-upon-Tyne, a man whom Count Apponyi in a private letter to Rechberg of 11 January 1863 was to describe as '*le plus chaud et actif de nos partisans.*' (HHStA, Administrative Registratur, F34, Handel, Grossbritannien, Karton 5.)
14 After his retirement from office Baron Thierry acted as a lobbyist for a group of British businessmen who wished to obtain a concession from the Austrian government for the establishment of an Anglo-Austrian bank. It was in this and not in any official capacity that he had come to England. See Constant Wurzbach, *Biographisches Lexikon des Kaiserthums Oesterreich*, vol. XLIV (Vienna, 1883), pp. 228ff.

the United Kingdom and Austria.[15] Having paid handsome compliments to Count Rechberg and his colleagues on their 'enlightened views' on these matters, the Prime Minister concluded with a broad hint at the political advantages Austria could expect to reap from a commercial agreement with Britain: 'I take the liberty of impressing upon our distinguished guest that by increasing the commercial intercourse between the two countries we are not only adding to the wealth, and happiness, and prosperity of both, but that we are to a very great degree cementing the political ties by which the two countries are bound together.'

Palmerston's public overtures to Vienna, which, we are told, 'made a sensation in Europe,'[16] were followed a few weeks later by a concrete and formal offer. Lord Bloomfield was directed to inform Count Rechberg that 'Her Majesty's Government would willingly agree to sign a treaty exactly similar to that concluded between France and Prussia, or with such modifications as might be agreed upon.'[17]

In making this proposal London appears to have seriously misjudged the intentions of the Imperial government. Rechberg replied at once in the negative to Bloomfield's communication, and his language was, if anything, more precise and explicit than it had been four months earlier.[18] 'He regretted to be obliged to say that, though the general principles of Free Trade had been adopted by the Cabinet and sanctioned by the Emperor last April, the continued opposition of the manufacturers and the disfavour with which the question was viewed in the *Reichsrath* made it useless to attempt any negotiation at this moment ... Pending an arrangement [with the *Zollverein*] it will be impossible for

15 *The Times* (London), 29 October 1862, p. 8.
16 Quotation from a paper read a few days after Palmerston's Southampton speech by Somerset Beaumont, MP, before the Newcastle Chamber of Commerce, as reported in the *Northern Daily Express*, 4 November 1862: HHStA, Administrative Registratur, F34, Handel, Grossbritannien, Karton 5 (newspaper clipping sent to Count Rechberg by the Austrian Consul-General in London).
17 Instruction for Bloomfield (draft) of 26 November 1862: PRO, FO 7/626.
18 Bloomfield's dispatch of 4 December 1862: PRO, FO 7/640. See also Rechberg's Instruction for Apponyi (draft) of the same date: HHStA, Politisches Archiv VIII, England, Karton 59.

[Austria], notwithstanding her ardent desire to promote closer commercial connections with England, to enter into negotiation with England.' For the rest, the British proposal to model an Anglo-Austrian convention on the Franco-Prussian treaty did not at all appeal to Vienna. Rechberg declared that 'unless greatly modified Austria could not adopt it; ... there was no reciprocity established in that treaty, and ... he believed the majority of the minor States of Germany would ultimately reject it.'

Bloomfield concluded this gloomy report with a few observations of his own. 'It seems to me,' he wrote, 'and I say so with deep regret, that the time is yet far distant when we may expect to be able to open commercial negotiations with Austria ... The opposition to any change in the present protective system is still so predominant in the Empire, and she considers her commerce with Germany so much more important than that with any other country, and is so bent on making an arrangement with the *Zollverein*, that until she sees her path more clearly marked out and that some decision is taken one way or the other as to the Franco-Prussian treaty, she will do nothing.'

Having met with yet another rebuff, the British government could only resign themselves to a policy of wait and see. Sooner or later Austrian relations with Prussia and the German Customs Union would become clarified, and attempts to persuade Vienna to revise its commercial policy might then be renewed with some hope of success. In the meantime London confined itself to raising some questions of tariff details through diplomatic channels. One such *démarche* was aimed at obtaining from Austria a reduction of the high duty – about 9s a barrel – charged on the importation of Scotch herrings. Verbal and written representations to that effect, begun as early as 1857 and renewed in 1862, had so far remained fruitless.[19] But Bloomfield and the Foreign Office seem

---

19 Instruction for Bloomfield (draft) of 12 June 1861: PRO, FO 7/605; Bloomfield's dispatch of 20 June 1861: PRO, FO 7/611; Bloomfield's note to Rechberg of 21 July 1861: HHStA, Administrative Registratur, F34, Handel, Grossbritannien, Karton 5; Bloomfield's dispatch of 25 July 1861: PRO, FO 7/612; note of the Austrian Ministry of Finance to the Ministry of Foreign Affairs of 23 August 1861: HHStA, Administrative Registratur, F34, Handel, Grossbritannien, Karton 5.

to have entertained some slight hopes that in the present situation, when Austria had refused to negotiate a general revision of her tariff, she might at least grant that minor concession. Once again, however, the effort proved unavailing. The British request, contained in Bloomfield's notes of 19 January and 20 May 1863,[20] was referred by Count Rechberg to the Minister of Trade for his opinion,[21] who rejected it out of hand.[22] Rechberg, whose influence was on the wane, seems to have accepted the negative verdict without demur. On 30 July 1863 Bloomfield informed the Foreign Office of this latest failure.[23] All he had been able to obtain was a vague assurance that the Imperial government would 'keep in mind the wish expressed by Her Majesty's government' and that they would 'give careful consideration to the question of a reduction of the present import duties on herring and cod' when, as was intended, the Austrian tariff would come in for re-examination in 1865.[24]

Yet another *démarche* was undertaken by Lord Bloomfield in February 1864; but it also proved futile. Instructed by the Foreign Office to reopen the ancient question of the export duty on rags,[25] the Ambassador called on Rechberg only to be put off again with a reference to the pending revision of the Austrian tariff.[26]

The Anglo-Austrian dialogue having reached a deadlock on the diplomatic plane, the more zealous devotees of Free Trade among British businessmen conceived of an alternative and, so they believed, more promising method of promoting a change in the protectionist policy of the Habsburg monarchy. If, as seemed obvious, the unyielding attitude of the Imperial authorities

20 HHStA, Administrative Registratur, F34, Handel, Grossbritannien, Karton 5.
21 Inter-departmental notes of 21 January and 23 May 1863: ibid.
22 Inter-departmental notes of 14 February and 4 July 1863 (Minister of Trade to the Ministry of Finance and Ministry of Finance to the Ministry of Foreign Affairs): ibid.
23 PRO, FO 7/654.
24 Note of the Austrian Ministry of Foreign Affairs to Bloomfield (copy) of 27 July 1863 (trans.): PRO, FO 7/654.
25 Instruction for Bloomfield (draft) of 13 February 1864: PRO, FO 7/664.
26 Bloomfield's dispatch of 23 February 1864: PRO, FO 7/667.

was due, first and foremost, to pressure from the industrial classes, it was the latter that needed persuading that they had little to fear and much to gain from a lowering of trade barriers. What seemed to be called for was a determined missionary effort, undertaken by men who understood the concerns and spoke the language of those whom they intended to convert. Businessmen rather than bureaucrats were the most effective apostles of the new faith; Chambers of Commerce might be listened to more readily by merchants and manufacturers than the Foreign Office.

It was with a view to creating an opportunity for a visit to Austria of such 'Free Trade missionaries' – an apt expression used by Count Rechberg[27] – that the British Chambers of Commerce urged their government to suggest to the Imperial authorities the appointment of a commission which would be charged with taking evidence from foreign businessmen regarding the expediency of lower duties. The Foreign Office seems to have hesitated for some time to take up this proposal; but when upon the failure of recent Prusso-Austrian negotiations at Prague in the spring of 1864 Vienna could be expected to re-examine her commercial relations with other countries, Lord Bloomfield received instructions to raise the question with Count Rechberg.[28] His representations were strongly supported by a Newcastle merchant of Hanseatic extraction, Mr Allhusen, a man who had all along taken an active interest in promoting closer commercial relations between Britain and Austria,[29] and who on this occasion had come to Vienna on a private fact-finding mission.[30] Rechberg, however, left no doubt that he was not prepared to act upon the suggestion. 'He feared,' Bloomfield reported, 'the moment was unfavourable for such an experiment. [The proposed commission] would have to be composed of delegates from the Austrian Chambers of Commerce, nearly all of whom were bent on main-

27 As reported by Bloomfield in his dispatch of 4 August 1864: PRO, FO 7/672
28 Instruction for Bloomfield (draft) of 18 May 1864: PRO, FO 7/664.
29 See his speech before the Newcastle Chamber of Commerce as reported in the *Northern Daily Express,* 4 November 1862: HHStA, Administrative Registratur, F34, Handel, Grossbritannien, Karton 5 (newspaper clipping).
30 Bloomfield's dispatch of 13 June 1864: PRO, FO 7/671.

taining the protective system; he therefore could see no present advantage in mooting the subject.'[31] But when asked by Bloomfield what his attitude would be if private individuals were to come to Vienna as advocates of Free Trade, the Foreign Minister replied 'that he should entirely approve of such visits; ... he would gladly see Vienna visited by English merchants who could explain to the commercial people of Austria the favourable working of [the English] system, and assist in breaking down their prejudices.'[32]

Earl Russell does not seem to have anticipated any objection to the British missionaries on the part of the Austrian government. Even before Bloomfield's dispatch of 4 August reached him, the Foreign Secretary had addressed a circular to the various Chambers of Commerce in Britain, suggesting that 'they should send delegates to Austria for the purpose of promoting Free Trade in that country.'[33] This proposal was received with alacrity. At the beginning of September the Associated Chambers of Commerce of the United Kingdom informed the Foreign Office that they had deputed 'three or four gentlemen, well acquainted with the leading branches of British commerce and in whose discretion the Association has full confidence ... to proceed to Vienna at an early date, accompanied by Mr. Allhusen, in order to carry out as far as possible the suggestion made by Her Majesty's Government that the commercial bodies in this country should enter into direct communications with similar associations in Austria, with a view of pointing out to them the advantages which would result to Austrian industry from the adoption of a system of Free Trade.[34] A number of letters of introduction sent to the Embassy in Vienna by the Foreign Office in the autumn of 1864 acquaint us with the names of some of the other delegates – Jacob Behrens, Esq.,[35] Mr Max Liebmann of Huddersfield,[36] Francis Prange, Esq., who had been chosen by the Liverpool

31 Bloomfield's dispatch of 4 August 1864: PRO, FO 7/672.
32 Ibid.
33 Instructions for Bloomfield (drafts) of 20 and 27 July 1864: PRO, FO 7/665.
34 Instruction for Bloomfield (draft) of 5 September 1864: PRO, FO 7/665.
35 Instruction for Bloomfield (draft) of 13 September 1864: PRO, FO 7/665.
36 Instruction for Bloomfield (draft) of 30 September 1864: ibid.

Chamber of Commerce,[37] and Mr Somerset Beaumont, MP.[38] The last-mentioned gentleman, who arrived at Vienna only on 21 December but at once assumed a leading role, was at the time President of the Newcastle Chamber of Commerce.[39]

Our documentation, unfortunately, does not indicate what specific contacts the members of the delegation managed to establish. Somerset Beaumont, whose social standing gave him entrée to Cabinet Ministers and high-ranking civil servants, is known to have argued the case of Free Trade in Vienna's official quarters.[40] (He had done so once before, in August 1862, in an interview with Count Rechberg.[41]) But the main efforts of the British delegates were aimed at convincing their Austrian fellow businessmen of the blessings of Free Trade. They carried in their briefcases a large number of beautifully printed copies of a memorandum drawn up by the Association of Chambers of Commerce of the United Kingdom and addressed to the Chambers of Commerce in the Austrian Empire[42]: as in the work of other mis-

37 Instruction for A.G.G. Bonar, Chargé d'Affaires (draft), of 30 November 1864: ibid. Francis Prange, a native of Austria, was a naturalized British subject and a resident of Liverpool. See the unidentified newspaper clipping enclosed in a report of the Austrian Consul at Liverpool to the Ministry of Foreign Affairs of 28 February 1864: HHStA, Administrative Registratur, F34, Handel, Grossbritannien, Karton 5.

38 Instruction for Bonar (draft) of [illegible] December 1864: PRO, FO 7/665.

39 See the report on a special meeting of that body in The Times of 25 October 1864 (newspaper clipping enclosed in a report of the Austrian Consul-General in London of 26 October 1864): HHStA, Administrative Registratur, F34, Handel, Grossbritannien, Karton 5.

40 See his letters to Earl Russell of 26 December 1864 (PRO, 30/22/45) and 31 December 1864 (British Museum, Add. Mss 44183, ff. 403–408v) and his letter to Bonar of 13 February 1865, enclosed in the latter's dispatch to Earl Russell of 14 February 1865: PRO, FO 425/79.

41 He reported on this interview in a speech before the Newcastle Chamber of Commerce on 3 November 1862. See above. p. 26, n. 16. See also his letter to Earl Russell of 31 December 1864: British Museum, Add. Mss 44183, ff. 403–408v.

42 A copy of this address was sent by the Austrian Consul-General in London to Count Wimpffen, the Austrian Chargé d'Affaires, who forwarded it to the Ministry of Foreign Affaires on 2 November 1864: HHStA, Administrative Registratur, F34, Handel, Grossbritannien, Karton 5.

sionaries preaching was supported by the distribution of edifying tracts among the infidels.

The British address, composed in almost faultless German, carefully avoided a magisterial tone. 'It would ill become an association like ours,' its authors protested, 'in addressing itself to a foreign country to lay claim to deeper insight, let alone to presume to teach similar bodies in Austria how best to promote the welfare of their constituents.'[43] But having made this disclaimer the authors felt free to offer their Austrian readers impressive evidence to show that the British economy, so far from being harmed, was prospering under a regime of Free Trade, whose adoption had at one time been strongly opposed in certain quarters with arguments very similar to those used by protectionist interests in other countries. Nor, they added, had experience borne out the prophecies of doom with which some French manufacturers had tried to dissuade their government from introducing, however cautiously and imperfectly, a policy of economic liberalism. Indeed, a glance at one of the statistical tables appended to the memorandum must have sufficed to convince the reader that the foreign trade of France, and particularly her exports to the United Kingdom, were increasing at a very satisfactory rate: the latter, valued at £12 million in 1857, had slightly more than doubled by 1863.

Though anxious to avoid giving offence to their Austrian readers the authors of the address could not refrain from drawing their attention to the stagnant volume of their country's foreign trade, particularly its trade with Britain. The reasons of this unsatisfactory state of affairs – all the more surprising in view of Austria's large, skilful, and industrious population, the high fertility of most of her regions, her mineral wealth, and her many other resources – were said to have been frequently discussed in the meetings of Britain's Chambers of Commerce; and there had been general agreement that the country's stagnation must

43 Ibid. (trans.); it has been thought preferable to retranslate the German version of the address (which, after all, was the one that was read by the Austrians) rather than quote from the original English text, which differed slightly from the German. A printed copy of the latter is to be found in HHStA, Administrative Registratur, F34, S.R., Karton 41, 2. Teil.

be attributed, in the main, to 'the fetters of an illiberal tariff.' The memorandum stated:

It would be an easy matter to accumulate proofs of the blessings of Free Trade and of the injurious effects of the opposite course. But the object of this address is not to propound an essay in Political Economy, far less to assume the invidious task of instructing foreign nations how to look after their own interests. We merely intend, respectfully, and in the most sincere and cordial spirit, to present to the Chambers of Commerce of the Austrian Empire the following questions for their serious consideration.

1. Whether the time has not arrived when the adoption of a policy of Free Trade, in the true interest of the business community, demands their earnest attention and deliberation.

2. If the Austrian Chambers of Commerce answer this question in the affirmative they are respectfully requested to find and suggest ways and means whereby a complete and thorough investigation of this important subject can be undertaken with a view to practical results.[44]

The appeal of the British businessmen to economic logic and statistical evidence met with a mixed reception in the Austrian press. To start with there was some positive response. The *Botschafter*, a Viennese journal which was known as a ministerial organ, and supposed especially to express the views of von Schmerling, the Minister of State, offered the British Chambers of Commerce its sincere appreciation of the 'service they have rendered to Austria by their address, by its eminently friendly spirit, and by the impulse it has given in Austria to direct public attention to the real causes of the unhealthy state of [her] economic affairs.' The paper characterized the language of that document as 'frank, warm, most reasonable, and worthy of being listened to and appreciated.'[45]

44 Ibid. (trans.).
45 Quoted by A.G.G. Bonar, the British Chargé d'Affaires at Vienna, in his dispatch of 17 November 1864: PRO, FO 7/674. See also the newspaper clippings enclosed in Bonar's dispatches of 22 and 23 December 1864, containing two more editorials published by the *Botschafter* in strong support of Free Trade: PRO, FO 7/674. Another Viennese journal, the *Debatte*, which was devoted to Hungarian interests, also advocated the adoption of a more liberal commercial policy. See Bonar's dispatch of 24 November, 1864: PRO, FO 7/674.

Other papers, however, reacted in a hostile manner to the British memorandum – unless they prudently refrained from offering their readers any editorial comment at all.[46] The *Austria*, for instance, an economic weekly edited by Lorenz Stein, the Professor of Political Economy in the University of Vienna,[47] in its issue of 21 November 1864 (vol. XVI, no. 47) dismissed the address with sneers and innuendoes. 'That address,' the paper wrote, 'proposes to teach Austria the great advantages of Free Trade. We are very grateful. But we frankly confess to our belief that we have already enough documents, theories and statistics to form, without those very able arguments, a tolerably clear opinion of those economic principles (which, after all, are of rather recent vintage even in old England, and not yet tested by long experience); we are also familiar with the way in which figures can be twisted in economic controversies. We should like nothing better than to see England take a lively, and above all an unprejudiced, interest in Austria and her industries. Nay we are entitled to demand this: for it seems to us, there has been no lack of prejudice. We expect first of all that England, if she addresses herself again to Austria, will for once consult the Austrian statistical tables, and recognize the progress we have made without adopting the new English system. We believe it will have to be admitted that a system of commercial policy that has achieved such success cannot be all that desperate after all.'

The wholly negative attitude of such a prestigious paper as

---

46 The *Volkswirth*, an economic weekly, in its issue of 11 November 1864 (vol. VII, no. 45), briefly reported on and quoted from the memorandum, but neither in this nor in any of the following numbers did it take any editorial stand on the merits of the document.

47 Lorenz Stein (later 'von Stein') was appointed to the Chair in 1855. His fame rested (and still rests) chiefly on his brilliant sociological study *Der Socialismus und Communismus des heutigen Frankreichs* (1842), which in its last edition (Leipzig, 1850/1) bore the title *Geschichte der socialen Bewegung in Frankreich von 1789 bis auf unsere Tage*. Stein's contributions to economics, on the other hand, remained insignificant. His *Lehrbuch der Volkswirthschaft* (Vienna, 1858), pp. 353ff., shows him an adherent of moderate Protection. On Lorenz von Stein see Palgrave's *Dictionary of Political Economy*, III, 474; *Encyclopedia of the Social Sciences*, XIV, 381; and *Handwörterbuch der Sozialwissenschaften*, X, 89ff. (with extensive bibliography).

the *Austria*, whose editor was one of the principal advisers of Baron Kalchberg, the acting Minister of Commerce,[48] did not augur well for the success of the British delegation. Nor did a vicious campaign in the Austrian press against its leading member, Somerset Beaumont.[49] A letter written to Newcastle by this gentleman in which he expressed his belief that 'our expectations will not be disappointed' had been given wide publicity by English newspapers. This public anticipation of a favourable outcome – wholly unwarranted as it turned out – embarrassed the Austrian government, and evoked highly critical comments from all the Viennese papers. The *Presse* in particular, under the heading 'An Itinerant Free Trader,' poured scorn on 'the notorious Member of Parliament, Mr. Somerset Beaumont,' and invited him 'to make himself acquainted with the appreciations of the majority of the Austrian Chambers of Commerce upon this subject.' This was a taunting reference to the fact that the Vienna Chamber of Commerce had quite recently drawn up a courteous but decidely negative reply to the address of their British colleagues which was certain to receive the approval of the other Chambers of Commerce of the Empire.[50]

A little later the British memorandum also elicited a negative response from an official Austrian source – a refutation, that is, of one of its assertions concerning the volume of Anglo-Austrian trade. In an interdepartmental note of 11 February 1865[51] the Ministry of Finance, to whom a copy of the British address had been communicated, informed the Ministry of Foreign Affairs that some of the statistical data assembled in the appendices to the memorandum were seriously misleading. Those figures, intended to illustrate the crippling effects of Austria's tariff on her foreign trade, were supposed to show that in terms of value Anglo-Austrian trade was only a small fraction of Britain's trade with the Hanse Towns (Hamburg, Bremen, and Lübeck). In 1858, for instance, the latter had received £11,577,000 worth of British imports, while the value of Austrian imports from the United

48 See Bonar's dispatch of 14 February 1865: FO 425/78.
49 See Bonar's dispatch of 11 January 1865 with enclosure: PRO, FO 425/78.
50 See Bonar's dispatch of 5 January 1865: PRO, FO 425/78.
51 HHStA, Administrative Registratur, F34, Handel, Grossbritannien, Karton 5.

Kingdom had amounted only to £1,596,000. Yet these data, the Ministry of Finance pointed out, by no means supported the conclusion they were meant to prove. They were extracted from British trade statistics, which classified exports, not according to their final destination, but according to the ports at which they were unloaded. Obviously the bulk of British cargoes discharged in the Hanse Towns was in transit, and quite a large portion was destined for Austria. Austrian imports from Britain, on the other hand, would be counted as such in the British statistics only if they reached their destination through one of the Austrian ports in the Adriatic. The memorandum, therefore, grossly underestimated the total value of British exports to Austria.

The Ministry of Foreign Affairs communicated these critical comments (which, however, merely expounded conclusions to be drawn from facts admitted by the authors of the British memorandum in a footnote) to Count Apponyi in London, who was instructed to pass them on to the Imperial Consul-General there, so that he might be in a better position to correct any erroneous conceptions of the British public concerning the volume of consumption of British commodities in Austria.[52]

Thus within a few weeks of their arrival in Vienna the missionary efforts of the delegates of the Chambers of Commerce had proved unavailing. Britain's Chargé d'Affaires, who seems all along to have taken a jaundiced view of the activities of those businessmen-turned-diplomats, attributed their failure to a lack of *savoir faire*. They had been too much in a hurry; they had asked too much; they had relied on 'public and loud agitation,' which could not 'be of service to us or advisable in Austria at the present moment,' and was 'only calculated to prove an embarrassment to the [Austrian] government and consequently an impediment to our interests.'[53] Somerset Beaumont, who was referred to by name as one of the culprits in Bonar's dispatch to the Foreign Office, had he been privy to it, would have keenly resented this criticism; but even he seems to have felt that it would be wise to entrust at least some of the work of commercial diplomacy once more to the skilful hands of professionals.

52 Instruction for Apponyi (draft) of 21 February 1865: ibid.
53 Bonar's dispatch of 11 January 1865: PRO, FO 425/78.

3
A Commission of Inquiry

British businessmen, though they were liable occasionally to complain of what they felt was inadequate attention to matters commercial on the part of the Foreign Office (see above, p. 15), never doubted that their Free Trade propaganda in Austria was merely preparatory and subsidiary to the work of the diplomats. The authors of the memorandum of the British Chambers of Commerce emphasized that 'the members of this Association, in addressing themselves directly to their *confrères* in Austria, rely on the goodwill and support of their respective governments; and while they proceed altogether independently of diplomatic negotiations, they hope by their efforts to promote such negotiations and bring them to a successful and mutually satisfactory conclusion.'[1]

The British business community must have come to appreciate the role of diplomacy even better when it became evident that their facile assumption – that their Austrian *confrères* would listen more readily to them than to government officials – had been entirely wrong. When the delegation of the British Chambers of Commerce met the stone wall of protectionist sentiment among Austrian manufacturers, its leading member, Somerset Beaumont, decided to gain instead the ear of the Austrian bureaucracy, and to enlist the support of the Foreign Office in his endeavour.

---

1 HHStA, Administrative Registratur, F34, Handel, Grossbritannien, Karton 5 (trans.).

A memorandum which Somerset Beaumont submitted to the Austrian authorities on 1 January 1865[2] clearly expressed his keen disillusionment with the attitude of the Austrian business community. 'The question of moderate or of high tariffs,' he declared, '[should] be considered with a view to the prosperity and welfare of the whole Empire of Austria, instead of being discussed by persons interested in the maintenance of an existing system, and who are rarely found ready to sacrifice personal advantages to the general good. The reports of the [Austrian] Chambers of Commerce[3] are proof of the undesirability of leaving the decision of important public questions to mere commercial associations.' Beaumont therefore suggested the appointment of an Anglo-Austrian commission of inquiry, 'composed of a few enlightened and impartial men' whose task it would be to examine some of the practical problems of transition which Austrian manufacturers would have to face if the country were to move from Protection towards Free Trade.

A stickler for protocol might have found it objectionable that a private individual should have presumed to offer gratuitous advice to a foreign government. But then Somerset Beaumont had a stake in the Austrian economy: he was a shareholder in the Anglo-Austrian Bank,[4] and seems to have also been 'engaged in railways in Austria.'[5] He was, moreover, the leading member of the deputation of the British Chambers of Commerce, whose visit to Vienna had been sanctioned by the Imperial government, and he may well have felt that he was entitled to a hearing. What was wholly unpardonable, however, was that Beaumont, in presenting his scheme of a mixed commission of inquiry to the Aus-

2 HHStA, Administrative Registratur, F34, S.R., Karton 41.
3 This reference is to reports which the Austrian government had earlier received on a projected tariff revision. All the Chambers of Commerce with the exception of those of Trieste, Budapest, Linz, and Fiume were more or less unfavourable to the government project. See Bloomfield's dispatch of 30 June 1864 with enclosures: PRO, FO 7/671.
4 The fact is mentioned in a letter of 27 February 1865 addressed to Earl Russell by Sampson S. Lloyd, the Chairman of the Association of Chambers of Commerce of the United Kingdom: PRO, FO 7/692.
5 This is what Mr. Allhusen told Edmund Hammond, the Under-Secretary in the Foreign Office; see the latter's minute of 20 February 1865: PRO, FO 7/692.

trian authorities, arrogated an official status: that plan, he stated in his memorandum, was submitted 'on behalf of Her Majesty's government.' The fact of the matter was that the gentleman from Newcastle had never been authorized to make that or any other proposal. Indeed, in a letter to Earl Russell[6] written only the day before he handed in his memorandum to the Austrians, he had obliquely complained that his efforts were hampered by his lack of official standing, and he had asked for a commission.

Beaumont's pressing request, which raised fundamental issues concerning the relationship between the world of business and the diplomatic service, caused Lord Russell some embarrassment. To be sure no Foreign Secretary, not even one who was a member of a Liberal government, which owed its power to the vote of the middle classes, could accept (and not very many businessmen are likely to have shared) the naive views advanced in a recent editorial of *The Times* which had asserted that 'the new era of diplomacy [had] fairly begun'; that 'Ambassadors and Secretaries of Legation will no longer be careful to interfere with royal marriages, to support a tottering Ministry, or to baffle schemes of territorial aggression'; that 'henceforth the business of a diplomatic agent will be to study the rise and fall of markets or the course of exchange, and to send home periodical reports on the commerce of our neighbours'; and that 'as a corollary to such a change *our Ministers abroad will take their instructions from Chambers of Commerce instead of the Foreign Secretary.*'[7]

Such extravagant claims could be dismissed. Yet it would not do to antagonize the business community by flatly refusing one of its spokesmen in the House of Commons the requested 'special mission' when, as he affirmed, success was within his grasp. On the other hand the Foreign Secretary must have been reluctant to set a precedent for admitting ambitious outsiders to the halls of the mighty through the tradesmen's entrance.

Earl Russell's carefully worded reply to Beaumont's letter[8] reflected his dilemma. He admitted that the latter, 'if [he were]

6 British Museum, Add. Mss. 44183, ff. 403–408v.
7 *The Times*, 25 October 1864, italics mine.
8 Earl Russell to Somerset Beaumont (draft), 3 January 1865: PRO, FO 7/692.

to negotiate must have, and be known to have, the confidence of the British government'; and he seemed to imply, by strictly defining the limits of his future powers, that Beaumont would eventually be given some authority. 'You cannot stipulate,' Russell warned him, 'to yield a shilling of the public revenue of this country without the express sanction of the Chancellor of the Exchequer. ... Every step taken must be submitted to the Board of Trade. ... You must communicate constantly, by word of mouth or in writing, with the Queen's Ambassador or *Chargé d'Affaires* at Vienna.' At this point, however, Russell's letter stopped abruptly: it did not contain any promise that the 'special mission' Beaumont had asked for would be forthcoming.[9]

Earl Russell clearly regarded this matter as one of great urgency and importance. He directed Edmund Hammond, the Undersecretary in the Foreign Office, to submit copies of Beaumont's letter and of his proposed answer to Gladstone and Lord Palmerston for comment;[10] and it was only after his colleagues had indicated their approval[11] that the Foreign Secretary authorized the dispatch of his reply to Beaumont.

Though Beaumont was not made a special envoy – it was only a month later that Russell authorized him 'to act conjointly with [Mr Bonar, the British Chargé d'Affaires] in carrying on communication with the Austrian government'[12] – he continued his lobbying activities at Vienna, calling on Ministers, either alone or in the company of Bonar;[13] and, like any other diplomatic agent, he would send reports to the Foreign Secretary.[14] Nor

9 This omission was not due to inadvertence. In a note to Edmund Hammond of 2 January 1865 Russell explained that he did not propose to give Beaumont a special mission, though such a step might become necessary later on: PRO, FO 7/692.
10 Earl Russell to Somerset Beaumont, 3 January 1865: PRO, FO 7/692.
11 Their notes are dated 3 January and 4 January 1865 respectively: PRO, FO 7/692.
12 Instruction for Bonar of 6 February 1865: PRO, FO 425/78.
13 Beaumont's conferences with Austrian Ministers are frequently mentioned in Bonar's dispatches, e.g., 16 January, 19 January, and 28 January 1865: PRO, FO 425/78.
14 Somerset Beaumont to Earl Russell, 12 January, 16 January, and 6 February 1865: PRO, 30/22/45 and PRO, 30/22/43.

was his *idée maitresse* – the joint commission of inquiry – lost sight of. The setting up of such a body, for which the French *enquête* before the *Conseil Supérieur* in 1860 provided a model,[15] had been proposed to Vienna once before, in May 1864, but the plan had been rejected by Count Rechberg (see above, p. 29). Now the matter was taken up again by the Foreign Office. On 17 January 1865 Bonar received orders 'to propose the appointment of a Joint Commission charged with the duty of examining the Austrian tariff.'[16]

This time the idea seemed to find favour with the Imperial government. Following a meeting of the Council of Ministers in which Baron Kalchberg reported on his talks with Bonar and Beaumont,[17] Count Mensdorff-Pouilly, who upon Rechberg's resignation the previous October had become Foreign Minister, on 9 February 1865 addressed a note to the British Chargé d'Affaires[18] informing him of the acceptance by his government of the British proposal, and inviting him to take the proper steps for the nomination of the English members of the commission. On 13 February the news of the impending appointment of the commission was given to the Austrian public in the official *Wiener Abendpost*.[19] The wording of the announcement was obviously designed to reassure the Protectionists. 'This Commission,' the paper stated, 'will merely confine itself to an examination into the commercial relations and intercourse of England and Austria, and to the attainment thereby, if possible, of a basis for establishing facilities of intercourse, and reductions in the tariff in the interest of the two countries.[20] This official emphasis on the limited terms of reference of the commission, however, does not seem to have

---

15 See Arthur L. Dunham, *The Anglo-French Treaty of Commerce of 1860 and the Progress of the Industrial Revolution in France* (Ann Arbor, 1930), pp. 135 ff.
16 PRO, FO 7/688 (draft). The instruction was repeated on 1 February 1865: PRO, FO 425/78.
17 HHStA, Kabinettsarchiv, Ministerratsprotokolle, 6 February 1865.
18 Enclosed in Bonar's dispatch of 9 February 1865: PRO, FO 425/78.
19 A translated extract of this article was enclosed in Bonar's dispatch of 13 February 1865: PRO, FO 425/78.
20 Ibid.

caused Bonar any misgivings; indeed he was jubilant. The news release, he wrote to Earl Russell, 'is the first act of open defiance thrown at the all-powerful protectionist phalanx in and out of the *Reichsrat*, and is therefore of the best augury for the ultimate success of the labours of the Commission.'[21]

Bonar's optimism was hardly justified, seeing that the Commission of Inquiry was to come 'under the direction of the Imperial Ministry of Commerce,'[22] that bureaucratic stronghold of Protection. Its head, Baron Kalchberg, who was to select the Austrian members of the commission and serve as its chairman,[23] probably did not even deserve the benefit of the doubt given him by Bonar, who, while complaining of his 'eternal hesitations,' still believed in his good intentions.[24] As for Professor Lorenz Stein, whom Kalchberg appointed his deputy and put in charge of the secretariat of the commission,[25] he had long since revised his earlier Free Trade convictions and accepted Friedrich List's arguments in favour of protection for 'infant industries' (see above, p. 34, n. 47).

The selection of the other Austrian members of the commission took some time. For one thing it was not easy to find Hungarians willing to serve, since most of them, in protest against Vienna's centralizing policies, had long ago sullenly withdrawn from all participation in Imperial affairs. It was only in response to a personal appeal by the Emperor that two Hungarian noblemen, the Counts Johann Barkoczy and Emil Dessewffy – the latter the President of the Budapest Royal Academy[26] – finally accepted a commission.[27] Nor, apparently, were Austrian (i.e., non-Hungarian) businessmen any too anxious to become (or remain) members of a body set up for the purpose of promoting the cause

21 Ibid.
22 Count Mensdorff's note of 9 February 1865: PRO, FO 425/78.
23 Ibid.
24 Bonar's dispatch of 13 February 1865: PRO, FO 425/78.
25 Kalchberg's note to Bonar of 13 February 1865: ibid.
26 See the article on Dessewffy in *Österreichisches biographisches Lexikon*, I, 180.
27 See R.B.D. Morier's memorandum of 30 March 1865, enclosed in William Hutt's dispatch to Earl Russell of 4 April 1865: PRO, FO 425/79.

of Free Trade. Two of them, the Barons Zoenobius Popp von Böhmstätten and Constantin von Reyer, having first accepted the appointment, soon changed their minds and tendered their resignations one day before the first meeting of the commission.[28] Two more of its members, Alfred Skene and Simon Winterstein, both prominent members of the opposition in the *Reichsrat*,[29] resigned a few weeks later.[30] Even before these resignations were handed in, Lorenz Stein, in a memorandum dated 12 April 1865 and addressed to Count Mensdorff,[31] commented on the reluctance of most of the Austrian members of the commission to take part in its activities. They are apt to refuse to participate, he wrote, 'partly so as not to contribute to a more liberal commercial course in Austria, partly with a view to creating difficulties for the government, partly because they do not wish to anticipate their vote in the Chamber of Deputies.'

The British government also encountered some difficulties before the membership of the commission was definitely settled: only their troubles were of a different nature. There can be little doubt that the Cabinet, as one of its critics remarked in retrospect, had been 'desirous to stamp upon [the Joint Commission] an official and diplomatic character to an extent which at first threatened even to exclude Mr. Beaumont from it.'[32] As a matter of fact on 7 February 1865 Earl Russell informed Bonar that the government intended to name only himself and 'a person from here' as their commissioners: he was to state this to Beaumont.[33] The latter, when apprised of this decision, must have been sorely vexed and disappointed; but he had no intention to take his exclusion lying down. On the eve of his departure from Vienna he addressed a long letter to Bonar in which he,

28 Their joint letter of resignation, dated 21 April 1865 and addressed to Kalchberg, is found in AVA, Präsidium des Handelsministeriums.
29 See Morier's memorandum of 30 March 1865: PRO, FO 425/79.
30 William Hutt's dispatch to Earl Russell of 1 June 1865: ibid.
31 HHStA, Administrative Registratur, F34, S.R., Karton 41, 2. Teil.
32 Mr Francis Prange in a speech given before the Liverpool Chamber of Commerce on 14 March 1865; unidentified newspaper clipping enclosed in a report of the Austrian Consul at Liverpool to Count Mensdorff of 16 March 1865: HHStA, Administrative Registratur, F34, Handel, Grossbritannien, Karton 5.
33 PRO, FO 425/78.

without explicitly announcing his candidacy, emphatically stated his conviction 'that men practically versed in commerce should rank among [the] members [of the Commission] ... Without this element ably and strongly represented in it ... the Commission will be able to effect but little good.'[34] Bonar passed this letter on to Russell without comment.[35] For a moment it seemed as if the Foreign Office would not yield an inch. On 20 February 1865 – by that time Beaumont's letter must have been in Russell's hand – Bonar was instructed to communicate to the Austrian government the names of three men appointed to represent Britain on the Joint Commission – that of William Hutt, Vice-President of the Board of Trade, his own, and that of R.B. Morier, Second Secretary to the British Embassy at Berlin.[36] Somerset Beaumont had again been passed over.

Meanwhile, however, some leading representatives of Britain's business community had been alerted by Beaumont. On 20 February one of his Newcastle friends, Mr Allhusen, having first spoken to William Hutt, called on Edmund Hammond, Undersecretary of Foreign Affairs, to protest against Beaumont's exclusion. He warned him of 'the strong feeling which would be excited in the Chambers of Commerce, whose delegates were to meet tomorrow, if Mr. S. Beaumont were not named a commissioner'; and he threatened that William Edward Forster, the Member for Bradford, 'would attend to the matter in the House of Commons.' He added that he was 'quite sure that the negotiation would fail if Mr. S. Beaumont was not on the Commission.' When Hammond replied that Beaumont would have an opportunity of appearing before the commission in his capacity as an expert witness, Mr Allhusen expressed doubts whether he would choose to do so

34 Beaumont's letter to Bonar of 13 February 1865: PRO, FO 425/79.
35 Bonar's dispatch of 14 February 1865: ibid.
36 Instruction for Bonar of 20 February 1865: PRO, FO 425/78. Morier was highly qualified for this position. He spoke German fluently and had a special knowledge of Austrian affairs, having served as Attaché at Vienna from 1853 to 1858. See Rosslyn Wemyss [i.e., Victoria Wemyss. Baroness Wester-Wemyss], *Memoirs and Letters of the Right Hon. Sir Robert Morier, G.C.B.* (London, 1911), I, 132ff.

'unless he was a commissioner.'[37] Beaumont's appointment to the commission was also strongly urged by the Association of Chambers of Commerce of the United Kingdom and its chairman, Sampson S. Lloyd,[38] who suggested in a letter of 27 February to Earl Russell that 'after the quasi-official sanction with which [Beaumont] has recently visited Vienna, his non-appearance during a future date of the negotiation might excite unfavourable surmises.'[39]

Exposed to all those pressures the Foreign Office decided to give in. Though Earl Russell in a dispatch to Bonar of 21 February 1865 had still expressed his reluctance to give Beaumont a commission, since 'his attention appears to have been more especially directed to one object of British industry – iron, whereas it is my duty to watch over and promote all interests alike,'[40] two days later he directed the Chargé d'Affaires to sound the Austrian government about increasing the number of British commissioners to four, adding that, should this be acceptable to Vienna, 'Her Majesty's government would be disposed to name Mr. Somerset Beaumont as the additional member.'[41] Having been informed by Bonar that the Imperial government had no objection,[42] Russell on 4 March 1865 issued a joint commission to Hutt, Bonar, Morier, and Beaumont.[43] One further change in the British membership of the commission occurred early in May, when Louis Mallet, one of the most gifted civil servants in the employ of the Board of Trade, who had served his apprenticeship on Richard Cobden's staff at Paris in 1860,[44] replaced Bonar.[45] Lord

37 Quoted from a minute in Hammond's handwriting in which he recorded the salient points of his interview with Allhusen, dated 20 February 1865: PRO, FO 7/692.
38 His correspondence with Earl Russell is to be found in FO 7/692.
39 Ibid.
40 PRO, FO 425/79.
41 Instruction for Bonar of 23 February 1865: PRO, FO 425/78.
42 Bonar's telegraphic dispatch of 24 February 1865: PRO, FO 425/79.
43 Draft in PRO, FO 7/693: the final text is printed in FO 425/79.
44 Dunnam, p. 294.
45 See the instruction for Lord Bloomfield of April 25 1865 (draft): PRO, FO 7/688, and the latter's dispatch of 4 May 1865: PRO, FO 7/690.

Bloomfield, who by that time had resumed his ambassadorial functions in the Austrian capital, never became a member of the commission.

William Hutt and Robert Morier arrived at Vienna late in March 1865.[46] On 29 March they had a first interview with Baron Kalchberg,[47] and on 6 April they were received by the Emperor in private audience.[48] As he was to do frequently in the months and years to come, Morier recorded the substance of those conversations, together with observations of his own, and had these memoranda transmitted to Earl Russell by William Hutt.[49]

Morier got the impression that Kalchberg, aware that the British had little if anything to offer in the way of tariff concessions, looked upon the Anglo-Austrian negotiations chiefly as a means of obtaining British capital for his country, more particularly funds for the construction of railways. He seemed to hope that the British government, in return for a reduction of duties, would give 'if not directly at least indirectly, ... an impulse to English enterprise in Austria.' Morier could only smile at such naiveté: he knew 'that the British government can as little direct the course which British capital should take as it can regulate the action of the tides.' But he was confident that, once Austrian trade and industry were liberated from 'the legislative dead weight which bears it down,' capital and enterprise would of themselves flow in through the flood-gates thus opened.[50]

While Baron Kalchberg's language appears to have been guarded, the Emperor conducted his audience with the British commissioners 'in a cordial and almost hearty manner.' He expressed his admiration for England's sound financial position and the way she had mastered the cotton crisis. Then, turning to the object of the Commission of Inquiry, Francis Joseph suggested

46 See Russell's telegram to Lord Napier (draft) of 6 March 1865 and Hutt's dispatch to Russell of 30 March 1865: PRO, FO 425/79.
47 Hutt's dispatch to Russell of 4 April 1865 with enclosure: ibid.
48 Hutt's dispatch to Russell of 10 April 1865 with enclosure: ibid.
49 Ibid.
50 Ibid.

to his interlocutors that they should proceed with care, since 'as yet the manufacturers of Austria were very far from seeing matters in the proper light.' The impression left upon Morier was that 'the Emperor took a personal interest in the questions to be discussed by the Commission; that he was inclined to take a favourable view of [the British] side of the argument; and that he expressed his interest in a frank, straightforward and unreserved manner.'[51]

The monarch was obviously well informed when he cautioned the British commissioners not to underestimate the strength of the protectionist forces in Austria. Kalchberg certainly saw to it that they were represented on the commission: it numbered among its members such well known Protectionists as Alfred Skene, a Moravian cloth manufacturer,[52] and Baron Constantin Reyer, a Trieste merchant, whom Kalchberg pretended to have mistaken for a Free Trader.[53] The latter, in a preparatory meeting of the Austrian commissioners held on 19 April 1865, 'in no measured terms' proclaimed his opposition to the very *enquête* in which he was supposed to take part;[54] and it soon became apparent that at least two or three other Austrian members of the commission shared his views. Even if they did not at once follow Reyer's example of resigning, they demonstrated their lack of interest by absenting themselves from the meetings.

Perhaps more ominous even than the apathy or hostility of some of the Austrian commissioners were certain implications of a statement made by Baron Kalchberg early in May before the Tariff Committee of the *Reichsrat*. In reply to a question the acting Minister of Commerce declared that the Imperial government intended the revised tariff, which was then before the House, to have some permanence: it would not be altered during the next two or three years at least. The British commissioners were taken aback. In giving this assurance, Lord Bloomfield pointed

---

51 Ibid.
52 See Wurzbach, xxxv, 53ff.
53 See Morier's memorandum of 20 April 1865, enclosed in William Hutt's dispatch to Russell of the same date: PRO, FO 425/79.
54 Ibid.

out to Mensdorff,[55] Kalchberg had prejudged the main issue the Joint Commission was about to examine, and had thus negated its very *raison d'être*.

For the rest the inquiry after a few meetings became bogged in procedural questions and an unmanageable mass of detail; and by the end of May 1865 the patience of the British commissioners was wearing thin. On 24 May, after yet another unprofitable session, William Hutt took occasion to express to Kalchberg his 'great dissatisfaction at the manner in which [their] affairs were going on,' only to be fobbed off with vague promises. Then a few days later, when he learnt from the newspapers that two more Austrian commissioners had withdrawn, Hutt 'saw clearly that Baron de Kalchberg's whole system had collapsed, and that it was perfectly idle to go on with it, or to attempt, with its damaged remains, to do that which [the commissioners] found impossible when it was whole and complete.'[56]

William Hutt at once consulted his colleagues, who concurred with his conviction that, if the purpose of the commission was to be achieved at all, its Austrian section must undergo a 'thorough reconstruction'; that it was to have 'fit and competent members, pledged to attend to its duties'; that the commission 'must have a more effective president than M. de Kalchberg'; that the subject of the *enquête* must be more limited and more clearly defined; 'and that all these things must be provided for at once.'[57] That same evening, at a reception given by Countess Mensdorff, Hutt found an opportunity of speaking to the Foreign Minister about the breakdown of the commission. He warned him that he 'could go on with it no longer; and that unless the Imperial government was at once ready with an effective remedy, [he] must return home, as [he] was not sent by the British government to Vienna to take part in a farce.'[58]

Hutt's complaints and similar, if more restrained, representa-

55 Bloomfield's note to Mensdorff of 9 May 1865 (trans.): AVA, Präsidium des Handelsministeriums.
56 Hutt's dispatch to Russell of 1 June 1865: PRO, FO 425/79.
57 Ibid.
58 Ibid.

tions on the part of Lord Bloomfield,[59] met with reassuring responses from Count Mensdorff. William Hutt in a dispatch to Earl Russell quoted him as saying that he considered his 'honour engaged to see justice done to the British government about the Commission.'[60] However, a special meeting of the Council of Ministers, convened at Mensdorff's request to discuss ways and means of reorganizing the commission, failed to reach a decision.[61] Apparently the Austrian Cabinet, which had all along been anxious to avoid giving the *enquête* an official character, was still reluctant to act upon Hutt's request that the commission be strengthened by the appointment of two or three persons of a 'high and responsible official position ... so that whatever may be [its] conclusions, Her Majesty's government may have the moral assurance that they will be shared in by the responsible advisers of the Austrian government.'[62]

Then, unexpectedly, the Austrians appeared to give in. On 7 June 1865 Mensdorff informed Bloomfield confidentially that he and his colleague von Plener had managed to obtain Baron Kalchberg's assent to a reconstruction of the commission.[63] He, Kalchberg, would remain its nominal head, but Prince Jablonowski, who had recently been named Vice-President,[64] would henceforth conduct its meetings. Baron Brentano, a high-ranking civil servant in the Ministry of Finance, whom Mensdorff described as 'a man of liberal commercial opinions,' was also to be made a member of the commission. Another 'man of enlightened opinions in questions of trade,' Herr von Schwarz, the Austrian Consul at Paris, had been invited by telegraph to serve on the commission as a representative of the Ministry of Foreign Affairs; but Mens-

59 See Bloomfield's dispatches of 31 May, 1 June, 3 June, 5 June (with enclosures), and 8 June 1865: PRO, FO 425/79.
60 Hutt's dispatch to Russell of 1 June 1865: ibid.
61 Bloomfield's dispatch to Russell of 3 June 1865: ibid.
62 Hutt's letter to Bloomfield of 5 June 1865: ibid.
63 Bloomfield's dispatch to Russell of 8 June 1865: ibid.
64 See Kalchberg's note to Mensdorff and von Plener of 15 May 1865 (draft), and Jablonowski's letter of acceptance of the same date: both AVA, Präsidium des Handelsministeriums. Karl Prince Jablonowski was a member of the Upper House and Vice-President of the Carl-Ludwigs Railway.

dorff was not sure of his acceptance, 'as he may be afraid of the unpopularity attending it.' The Ministry of Finance was to be represented by *Ministerialrat* Peter and the Ministry of Commerce by Herr Parmentier or by 'some other man of liberal opinions.'

It all would have sounded very promising had it not been for Mensdorff's concluding remarks which, though they need not necessarily be suspected of ominous implications, could well be understood to portend yet another attempt on the part of the Austrian protectionists to sabotage or at least to delay the work of the commission. 'He apprehended,' Mensdorff told Bloomfield, 'it would be extremely difficult to get the machine in good working order at the present moment, on account of the advanced state of the season. ... He thought, therefore, it might be advisable to adjourn the labours of the Commission for a couple of months, provided Her Majesty's government had no objection to so doing.'[65]

London could, of course, have objected to an adjournment; but such a protest would hardly have served any purpose. Lord Bloomfield consequently was instructed to inform the Austrian authorities of his government's acquiescence;[66] and on 21 June 1865 William Hutt received permission to leave Vienna at the end of the month.[67] Count Mensdorff seems to have been pleasantly surprised at London's unconditional acceptance of his proposal. With an almost audible sigh of relief he informed his colleague Kalchberg that the British government had not even insisted that the commission should be reconstituted before its adjournment, let alone that the new body should hold an inaugural meeting.[68] William Hutt, however, was profoundly disappointed. 'I had hoped,' he wrote to Lord Bloomfield, 'on leaving Vienna not only to carry with me the promise of a reconstruction of the Commission, but to have seen the act of reconstruction completed,

65 Bloomfield's dispatch to Russell of 8 June 1865: PRO, FO 425/79.
66 Instruction for Bloomfield of 13 June 1865: ibid.
67 Earl Russell's instruction for Hutt of 21 June 1865: ibid.
68 Mensdorff's note to Kalchberg of 26 June 1865: AVA, Präsidium des Handelsministeriums.

and to have assisted at one sitting at least of the reconstructed body at which the programme of its future operations might have been definitely laid down; and that I should thus have been able personally to report to Her Majesty's government that, however unsatisfactory the past had been, we had at least a distinct object for our future labours.'[69] As it turned out there was no need to draw up a programme for the future operations of the commission: it was never to meet again. The expediency of terminating its proceedings altogether, or at least suspending them for three or five years, had been argued as early as May 1865 in a policy paper drawn up by Baron Max von Gagern, the head of the commercial section in the Austrian Ministry of Foreign Affairs.[70] One can hardly avoid suspecting that the Austrians had already made up their mind to disband the commission when they were still talking about its reconstruction after a two months' adjournment. Soon afterwards, however, the need for subterfuges disappeared. When Austria offered to negotiate a treaty of commerce with Britain (see below, p. 52), Count Mensdorff in a conversation with Bloomfield roundly declared that he saw no necessity for re-assembling the commission. His government, he averred, objected to the important character which it had assumed, and it was so unpopular with the public in Austria that it might tend rather to obstruct than to advance the reduction of the tariff. The object of the two governments, he added, would be attained equally well by the mere appointment of experts to decide technical details connected with the treaty which he proposed to negotiate.[71] A few weeks later when the Austrian Chargé d'Affaires in London informed Lord Russell officially that 'the Imperial

---

69 Hutt's letter to Bloomfield of 24 June 1865: PRO, FO 425/79.

70 This memorandum is unsigned and undated. Its authorship can be inferred from the fact that the draft (HHStA, Administrative Registratur, F34, Sonderreihe Karton 41, 2. Teil) is in Gagern's handwriting. A copy of this document was obtained 'in the strictest confidence,' probably from Gagern himself, by Bloomfield, who sent a translation to Earl Russell (see Bloomfield's 'most confidential' dispatch of 15 June 1865 with enclosure: PRO, FO 425/79). Bloomfield had already referred to this memorandum in his dispatch to Russell of 1 June 1865 (ibid.), which gives a *terminus ante quem* for its origin.

71 Bloomfield's dispatch to Russell of 17 August 1865: PRO, FO 425/80.

government are desirous that the International Commission ... should not assemble again,'[72] the British agreed to the Austrian proposal without indulging in useless recriminations.[73]

The commission, which had thus come to an inglorious end, had accomplished very little: it had met only seven times, and only three of those meetings had been for the purpose of receiving the evidence of witnesses.[74] A change in the Austrian personnel of the commission such as William Hutt had envisaged might have brought about some improvement in its proceedings; but the general atmosphere of mutual distrust which surrounded the *enquête* could hardly have been dispelled. Under these circumstances the British, though they must have felt cheated and frustrated, may have had few regrets about the demise of the commission. They now pinned their hopes on the proffered negotiation of a commercial treaty which, as Mensdorff pointed out, could 'be commenced at once and concluded, if possible, without publicity and before a violent protectionist agitation were raised against it.'[75]

72 Russell's instruction for Bloomfield of 6 September 1865: ibid.
73 Bloomfield's dispatch to Russell of 18 October 1865: ibid. The letters notifying the Austrian members of the commission of its termination were dated 13 October 1865: AVA, Präsidium des Handelsministeriums.
74 Hutt's dispatch to Russell of 27 June 1865: PRO, FO 425/80.
75 Bloomfield's dispatch to Russell of 18 October 1865: ibid.

4
A treaty at last

The prediction made by Lord Bloomfield in 1862 (see above, p. 27), that Austria would not enter into commercial negotiations with Britain before her relations with the German Customs Union were settled one way or the other, proved correct. Such a *dénouement*, however, was slow in coming. To be sure, by 1864 it was obvious that Austria's prolonged efforts to detach the smaller German States from Prussia had failed. Prussia had brought her recalcitrant associates in the *Zollverein* to heel, and, given her fixed intention to keep Austria out, the latter's prospects of ever gaining admission to the Union were getting decidedly dim. In these circumstances Vienna began seriously to cast about for alternative courses.

Proposals based on a realistic assessment of the situation were offered the Austrian government by one of their most competent official advisers, Baron Carl von Hock,[1] in a memorandum dated 4 March 1864.[2] He argued that Austria ought to abandon the unattainable goal of a closer connection with Germany: in future her commercial relations with the Customs Union should be governed solely by her economic interests. Instead of pursuing the will-o'-the-wisp of union with the *Zollverein* the Habsburg

1 Hock was *Sektionschef* (Deputy Minister) in the Ministry of Finance; see *Österreichisches biographisches Lexikon*, II, 346.
2 HHStA, Administrative Registratur, F34, Sonderreihe, Karton 41, 2. Teil.

monarchy had better start negotiations with its leading members – Prussia, Bavaria, and Saxony – with a view to concluding an ordinary treaty of commerce. Such a convention should provide above all for the continuance or extension of certain mutually advantageous arrangements concerning the border traffic between Austria and the *Zollverein*, such as the duty-free exportation and importation of goods for processing (*Veredelungsverkehr*), and cooperation in the customs administration and the prevention of smuggling (*Zollkartell*). As for tariff concessions, Austria should neither claim, nor indeed expect, any; on the contrary, she ought to be prepared to meet pressing demands on the part of the *Zollverein* for a reduction of her own import duties. Indeed, 'Austria, for the most serious political, fiscal and economic reasons, cannot isolate herself from the general movement towards Free Trade, which has spread from the West of Europe right up to her own borders, without inviting the enmity of those States, without suffering grievous losses of customs revenue, without harming her trade, and without surrendering her industry to the monopoly power of a few.'[3] Baron Hock added to his persuasive plea for liberalization a recommendation to start similar negotiations with France and, 'if politically expedient,' with England, as soon as a basic understanding with the German Customs Union was reached.

The cardinal point of Hock's program – his advocacy of efforts to reach a commercial agreement with the *Zollverein* – was approved by the government. A decision to that effect was reached in principle by the Council of Ministers in July and confirmed by them in a later meeting held on 12 December 1864.[4] Hock himself was charged with the conduct of the negotiation at Berlin, which led to the signature, on 11 April 1865, of a treaty of commerce with the German Customs Union (see below, p. 59). Not all of Hock's ideas, however, were accepted by the Council of Ministers. His proposal to enter into commercial negotiations

3 Ibid. (trans.)
4 HHStA, Kabinettsarchiv, Ministerratsprotokolle. The vote taken in July is referred to in the minutes of a Council meeting held on 10 December 1864 (ibid.). The minutes of the July meeting seem to be lost.

with France, sharply criticized by Baron Kalchberg, the acting Minister of Commerce, and only half-heartedly endorsed by Count Mensdorff and the *Staatsminister* (Premier) von Schmerling, was left in abeyance.[5] The idea of starting similar negotiations with Britain, guardedly advanced by Hock in his memorandum of 4 March 1864, was dismissed even more summarily by the Council of Ministers when it appeared that the author himself no longer stood by his original proposal. 'A negotiation with England,' the minutes of a meeting held on 12 December 1864 report him to have told the Ministers, 'is absolutely impossible,' seeing that Austria had nothing to offer with which to elicit reciprocal concessions.[6]

Confronted with conclusive evidence that support for an Anglo-Austrian negotiation was totally lacking in the Council of Ministers the historian is at a loss to explain how at that very moment it was possible for Somerset Beaumont in his correspondence with Earl Russell to voice nothing but optimism regarding the prospects of a commercial treaty. 'M. de Schmerling,' he wrote to the Foreign Secretary on 31 December 1864, 'who weighs his words and is known to act in complete agreement with Count Mensdorff, [told me] ... that the government were determined to make a treaty with England, that there was no reason for delay. ... I have more than once, during former visits to Vienna, seen M. de Schmerling; I never recollect him so emphatic and without hesitation. ... I ... have only to reiterate my conviction that the obtaining of a good treaty of commerce now entirely depends on the course which shall be adopted by the English government.'[7] To be sure, in his next letter, written on 12 January 1865, Beaumont sounded a somewhat more sober note, admitting that renewed hopes of obtaining some concessions from Prussia had caused Vienna 'for the present [to] keep quite quiet in negotiations with other countries.'[8] But only four days later the volatile gentleman from Newcastle resumed his sanguine tone. 'Your

5 HHStA, Kabinettsarchiv, Ministerratsprotokolle, 10 and 12 December 1864.
6 Ibid.
7 British Museum, Add. Mss 44183, ff. 403–408v.
8 PRO, 30/22/45.

Lordship need have no apprehension of [my] negotiations not resulting in a liberal treaty of commerce, if the British government express an unmistakable wish in the matter.'⁹ Can we assume that Beaumont, anxious to persuade Russell to give him official status, was guilty of deliberate misrepresentation? Or was he himself the victim of an optimistic illusion, created by suave and ambiguous statements of Austrian Ministers and civil servants?

How much credence Earl Russell was prepared to give to Beaumont's communications it is difficult to judge. But the record shows that in one case at least, and that an important one, he was sufficiently impressed by Beaumont's assessment of the situation to act upon it. When he was told that in the event of a sudden breakdown of the Berlin negotiation the Austrian government might 'at once propose to the British government the negotiation of a treaty of commerce,' the Foreign Secretary immediately sent a draft of such a treaty to the British Chargé d'Affaires in Vienna with instructions to communicate it at the proper moment to the Austrian authorities.¹⁰

In carrying out this directive Bonar had to use discretion. Unlike Beaumont he had no doubt that the Austrian government were determined to submit their tariff to an examination by the Joint Commission of Inquiry before conceding a general reduction of import duties under a treaty of commerce. A proposal *to start with a treaty* setting an upper limit to the duties levied under the Austrian tariff (such as was envisaged under Article II of the British draft), Bonar was sure, would be unacceptable to Vienna.¹¹ How touchy the Austrians were in this respect was shown just then. Having been apprised of a news item in the London *Times*, according to which the Vice-President of the Board of Trade was about to leave England for the purpose of negotiating an Anglo-Austrian treaty of commerce, Count Mensdorff and Baron von Gagern expressed their government's resentment of this report to Bonar, and the *Botschafter*, a semi-official news-

9 Ibid.
10 Instruction for Bonar of 6 February 1865: PRO, FO 7/688 (draft).
11 Bonar's dispatch of 14 February 1865: PRO, FO 425/78.

paper, published a *démenti*.[12] In view of Vienna's obvious reluctance to listen to any proposal aimed at negotiating a treaty at this stage, Bonar was well advised not to follow Russell's instructions of 6 February to the letter. He refrained from communicating the British draft officially to the Imperial government; instead he 'confidentially' handed over a copy of the document to Baron Max von Gagern, a high-ranking official in the Ministry of Foreign Affairs,[13] who was of a liberal persuasion and favoured an early treaty with England.[14]

If, as has just been shown, Earl Russell was misled by Beaumont's confident reports from Vienna, the Imperial Ministers were given an equally unsound account of British intentions by one of their colleagues. On 6 February, the very same day when Russell dispatched that draft to Bonar, Baron Kalchberg assured them that Beaumont and Bonar were not urging the conclusion of a treaty by any means, and that according to the latter Lord Russell, too, was perfectly satisfied with a Joint Commission of Inquiry whose function would be purely exploratory.[15] This simply was not true. Indeed, in an instruction for Lord Bloomfield Earl Russell was to make it abundantly clear 'that it would be of no use to appoint a Commission unless it was intended to reduce the [Austrian] tariff, and further that it would be of no use to appoint a Commission unless the result were to be a treaty of commerce with Great Britain.'[16]

If the Austrian Ministers had let themselves be persuaded by Kalchberg's assessment of British policy, they must have been

12 Bonar's dispatches (commercial nos. 17 and 22) of 13 and 14 February 1865: PRO, FO 7/689. The British government in a telegram to Bonar of 13 February 1865 expressed their regret for the erroneous report: PRO, FO 7/689 (draft).
13 The exact date on which Gagern received the draft cannot be ascertained. In a note to Lord Bloomfield of 2 April 1865 the Baron merely speaks of 'le projet de traité de commerce à moi confidentiellement remis par M. Bonar, il y a quelques semaines.' (Draft in HHStA, Administrative Registratur, F34, Sonderreihe, Karton 41, 1. Teil.)
14 See below, pp. 60f.
15 HHStA, Kabinettsarchiv, Ministerratsprotokolle.
16 Instruction for Bloomfield of 24 May 1865: PRO, FO 425/79.

not a little surprised when, only two months later, Lord Bloomfield (who in the meantime had returned to his post in Vienna) addressed a note to Count Mensdorff, requesting the Imperial government 'to consider the proposition of Her Majesty's government [i.e., the *projet* of a treaty of commerce] *as officially communicated*.'[17]

As might have been foreseen, Mensdorff's reply,[18] concerted in a hastily convened meeting with his colleagues von Plener and Baron Kalchberg, was negative. It was only too easy for him to argue that it would be improper to enter into negotiations, let alone conclude a treaty of commerce, at a moment when the Joint Commission of Inquiry, set up to examine the economic implications of such a convention, had not even started its deliberations, and when a revised tariff had just been laid before the *Reichsrat*. However Mensdorff left the door ajar. He hinted that Austria would eventually agree to a maximum rate of 20 per cent *ad valorem* for her import duties, and offered to continue informal discussions with Bloomfield and Hutt. The minutes recording the substance of one of these *pourparlers* between Baron Max von Gagern and the British[19] make it clear that the latter would have been satisfied, for the time being, with a binding promise from the Imperial government to make that maximum the basis for a future treaty, and to agree to a most-favoured-nation clause. But two British demands of long standing were not forgotten: Bloomfield and Hutt expressed their hope that Austria would see her way to lowering her export duty on rags and her import duty on salt fish. In return for such Austrian concessions, they gave to understand, Britain would lift her import duties on wood, especially staves, and possibly also abolish the trifling registration fee which was still collected from importers of grain.

---

17 Bloomfield's dispatch to Russell of 6 April, 1865: ibid. See also Baron Gagern's note to Bloomfield (draft) of 2 April and the latter's reply of 3 April 1865: both in HHStA, Administrative Registratur, F34, Sonderreihe, Karton 41, 1. Teil.

18 Mensdorff's note to Bloomfield of 6 April 1865: PRO, FO 7/689. An English translation of this note was enclosed in Bloomfield's dispatch of the same date: PRO, FO 425/79.

19 HHStA, Administrative Registratur, F34, Sonderreihe, Karton 41, 2. Teil. The meeting in question took place on 11 April 1865.

Meanwhile on 11 April 1865 Austria's treaty of commerce with the *Zollverein* had been signed at last (see above, p. 54), and the road to similar conventions with England and France seemed to be open. That the Habsburg monarchy, for political as well as economic reasons, would, sooner or later, have to regulate its commercial relations with the Western Powers in the form of treaties few Austrians could have doubted. But the powerful protectionist lobby in Vienna and their sympathizers in the councils of the government were determined to delay the start of negotiations. They reasoned, correctly, that the new tariff recently submitted to the *Reichsrat*, once it had received parliamentary sanction, would have to remain unaltered for some time to come. Therefore, having thus tied their hands, the government in future negotiations with Britain and France would happily be prevented from making any concessions involving a further scaling down of the reduced duties established under the revised tariff. This was admitted, if only by implication and with certain qualifications, by Baron Kalchberg when, replying to questions addressed to the Ministry by members of the Tariff Committee of the *Reichsrat*, he stated in the name of the government that the new tariff should indeed be regarded as final (see above, p. 47).

Kalchberg's statement, while it pleased the Protectionists and undoubtedly confirmed them in their desire to see the start of negotiations with Britain postponed until the tariff was passed through the *Reichsrat*, was read by Lord Bloomfield with some alarm. As he pointed out in his note to Mensdorff of 9 May 1865,[20] the labours of the Joint Commission of Inquiry, which was set up for the specific purpose of preparing the way to an Anglo-Austrian treaty of commerce, would be altogether nugatory if, as would appear, the Imperial Ministry of Commerce had made up its mind not to allow any changes in the tariff, whatever the verdict of the commission.

Count Mensdorff almost certainly was in favour of accommodating the British. Like his predecessor in the Ministry of Foreign Affairs he had to pay heed to public opinion in Britain, which expected Austria to undertake a long overdue reform of

20 HHStA, Administrative Registratur, F34, Sonderreihe, Karton 41, 2. Teil.

her commercial policy. Yet during his first months in office Mensdorff, having little knowledge of, and probably not very much interest in, matters economic, seems to have done little to make his views prevail over those of Kalchberg and his supporters in the Cabinet. As Somerset Beaumont put it in one of his letters to Earl Russell: 'Count Mensdorff gives an intelligent consideration to every question submitted to him; but perhaps from being a military man and not having had commercial subjects brought much before him hitherto, His Excellency hardly appreciates a proposal of a treaty of commerce as you would yourself.'[21]

However by the end of May 1865 Mensdorff could no longer overlook the growing irritation of the British representatives in Vienna with Kalchberg's incompetent direction, not to say wilful obstruction, of the Joint Commission of Inquiry. Their sense of frustration was expressed by Bloomfield in his testy note of 9 May and in even more forceful language by William Hutt in an interview with Mensdorff on 28 May (see above, p. 48). At this juncture Mensdorff at long last seems to have decided to put an end to a policy of evasion and tergiversation which threatened to poison Anglo-Austrian relations. No man in Mensdorff's Ministry was better qualified to marshal the arguments in favour of a policy of candour and conciliation than Baron Gagern; and it was he who was charged with the drawing up of a memorandum[22] to be placed before the Council of Ministers.

Gagern produced a remarkable document – remarkable not so much for its perfectly reasonable recommendations (which, in a nutshell, envisaged no more than an immediate start of serious commercial negotiations with France and England) as for its fanciful vision of a much more radical alternative. For a moment Gagern permitted himself to speculate on the possibility of Austria's 'outflanking Prussia' by resolutely adopting Free Trade in its entirety. If this were done England's goodwill would be won.

21 Beaumont's letter of 16 January 1865: PRO, 30/22/45.
22 Draft in HHStA, Administrative Registratur, F34, Sonderreihe, Karton 41, 2. Teil. Authorship and date of this document and the curious fact that a copy of it found its way into the British embassy are discussed above, p. 57, n. 13.

Moreover, 'on such a basis a complete economic plan could be agreed upon whereby, not indeed the English government, but the monied powers of the City could be called upon to help with the restoration to soundness of the Austrian finances. In this case ... the Commission of Inquiry would have to be carried on with greater earnestness and energy than hitherto, and the postulated grand plan would have to be prepared by a Minister thoroughly dedicated to the principles of Free Trade.' Gagern, of course, cannot for a moment have expected the Council of Ministers to consider, let alone approve, his 'grand plan.' Indeed, he himself dismissed it with a shrug of resignation. 'In the present state of affairs such a possibility does not appear to exist.'

However Gagern's more sober recommendation – to honour the promises given the Western Powers and start treaty negotiations forthwith – seemed to have a good chance of finding favour with the Cabinet. Indeed so confident was Count Mensdorff of its acceptance that he did not even await the decision of his colleagues. Two days before the special meeting of the Council of Ministers summoned to discuss Gagern's memorandum[23] he suggested to Lord Bloomfield that 'without waiting for the conclusion of [the] labours [of the Joint Commission of Inquiry] we might perhaps at once turn our thoughts to the question of a treaty.'[24] But Mensdorff did not have his way. After the meeting of the Cabinet he had to inform the British Ambassador that his colleagues 'were indisposed to take any immediate decision in the matter'[25]; and some days later Bloomfield reported to London that 'the great difficulties which Count Mensdorff has had to contend with in the Cabinet ... have forced him to abandon the project [of immediate negotiations].'[26]

Earl Russell showed his usual patience with Vienna's vacillation. He confined himself to the bland statement that 'Her Majesty's government still hope[d] to concur with that of Austria in

23 The minutes of this meeting, which was held on 2 June 1865 (see Bloomfield's dispatch of 1 June 1865: PRO, FO 425/79), seem to be lost.
24 Bloomfield's dispatch of 31 May 1865: ibid.
25 Bloomfield's dispatch of 3 June 1865: ibid.
26 Bloomfield's dispatch of 15 June 1865: ibid.

framing a treaty of commerce before the end of the year.'[27] When Bloomfield conveyed this message to Mensdorff he received the following reply. 'The Imperial government will always maintain the prerogative of the Crown to make treaties, ... and will also reserve to themselves the right of determining the proper time of negotiating such treaties.'[28] Taken out of its context this declaration would have sounded like a snub. But it was nothing of the sort; on the contrary, it implied a disavowal of Kalchberg's statement before the Tariff Committee of the *Reichsrat* which had provoked Bloomfield's anxious inquiry of 9 May 1865 (see above, p. 59), and was doubtless intended to reassure the British.

Mensdorff's renewed optimism about the chances of an Anglo-Austrian treaty must have been due to his knowledge that the days of the Schmerling government, with its strong representation of Protectionists, were already numbered. Rumours to that effect had even reached the ears of William Hutt, who in his dispatch of 27 June 1865 was able to tell Earl Russell that there were 'strong grounds for hoping that [before long] changes will have taken place which will enable the Austrian government to unite in a clear and consistent policy, and that such a policy may be in harmony with the objects which Her Majesty's government will have in view.'[29] He was referring to the impending dismissal of Schmerling's *soi-disant* liberal Cabinet and its replacement by a conservative government under the premiership of Count Belcredi.[30]

Most Englishmen, had they read Hutt's report, would have been puzzled by his assumption that the appointment of a conservative Cabinet in Austria would improve the prospects of Free Trade. But men familiar with the political scene in the Habsburg monarchy fully understood the apparent paradox. This is how Robert Morier, one of the British members of the Joint Commission of Inquiry, explained it in a letter to his father: 'Here, as

27 Instruction for Bloomfield of 13 June 1865: ibid.
28 Mensdorff's note to Bloomfield of 21 June 1865, enclosed in the latter's dispatch of 22 June 1865: ibid.
29 Hutt's dispatch of 27 June 1865: PRO, FO 425/80.
30 The change of government took place on 27 July 1865.

everywhere else abroad, the conflict underlying all other conflicts is that between the bourgeois and the privileged class; – now, the bourgeoisie and the manufacturing and industrial classes are identical, and whereas with us free trade was the rallying cry of the Liberals, and protection that of the privileged classes, we have here exactly the reverse, free trade being supposed to lie only in the interests of the landowners, and protection being the class cry of the Liberals, who represent the middle classes.'[31]

While William Hutt seems to have believed 'that the commercial policy of the [Austrian] Empire [was] the Alpha and Omega of the actual ministerial crisis'[32] his fellow commissioner clearly recognized that the Anglo-Austrian negotiation would be only a minor concern of the new Cabinet.[33] Quite apart from the intractable constitutional matters, one of the most pressing problems the new Premier, Count Belcredi, and his colleagues had to face was the desperate state of the Austrian finances.[34] The fiscal year, it was found, would end with a deficit of 80 million Florins, exceeding the budgetary estimates by 50 million. Direct taxes were seriously in arrears, and a large part of the current revenue was preempted for payments of interest on the national debt. So depleted were the public coffers that the new government, unable to scrape up enough money to pay the salaries due to their employees on August 1, were forced to raid the *Stadter-*

31 Rosslyn Wemyss [i.e., Victoria Wemyss, Baroness Wester-Wemyss], *Memoirs and Letters of the Right Hon. Sir Robert Morier, G.C.B.* (London, 1911), II, 5. Morier's was the kind of generalization Richard Cobden and John Bright used to indulge in during their agitation for the repeal of the Corn Laws. Actually, neither in England nor in Austria was the correlation between class and economic creed all that close. There were not a few noble landowners in the Habsburg monarchy who, being interested in iron mines and other industrial enterprises, were found in the Protectionist camp. Nor were all members of the Austrian bourgeoisie out of sympathy with the principles of Free Trade. Still, the main lines of Morier's sketch were drawn correctly.

32 Morier's letter to Russell of 14 July 1865: ibid., p. 8.

33 Ibid.

34 See Adolf Beer, *Die Finanzen Oesterreichs im XIX. Jahrhundert* (Prague, 1877), pp. 332ff; Lawrence D. Steefel, 'The Rothschilds and the Austrian Loan of 1865': *The Journal of Modern History*, VIII (1936), 27ff., and Bertrand Gille, *Histoire de la maison Rothschild* (Geneva, 1967), II, 439ff.

weiterungs Fond, a special fund set up for the purpose of providing the capital for new public buildings.

The need for yet another large loan was pressing. But it was clear that the domestic money market was ill equipped for such a credit operation: the money would have to be obtained abroad. The intentions of the Austrian government must soon have become known in London; for early in August Somerset Beaumont, acting as the agent of Messrs Baring and Glyn, set out for Vienna, where he was received by the Emperor and the leading members of the new Cabinet.[35] He was informed that the Imperial government wished to negotiate a loan in the London money market, and Count Larisch, the Minister of Finance, gave him authority 'to make the terms of the proposed loan known to some of our great capitalists.'[36] The Austrian government, he was told, required at once a sum of £15 million which, if the loan were issued at 75, would be realized by contracting for £20 million.[37] Reporting to Earl Russell on Beaumont's talks, Lord Bloomfield did not specify the interest rate at which the loan might be floated; but he intimated that the Austrian government, in its anxiety to obtain money, had offered such favourable terms as left no doubt in Beaumont's mind that they would be acceptable.[38]

However Beaumont was not concerned about the financial aspects of the transaction alone. Determined as always to promote Free Trade, he did not hesitate to exploit the fiscal predicament of the Austrian government for that end. He warned them 'that they must never expect to effect a large loan in London unless he were empowered to show confidentially to the leading commercial men some document proving that Austria was serious in her intention to remove restrictions from trade.'[39] Yielding to Beaumont's pressure, Count Mensdorff on 12 August actually

---

35 Bloomfield's dispatch of 10 August 1865: PRO, FO 425/80. See also Beaumont's letter to Lord Clarendon of 12 August 1865: Bodleian Library, M.S. Clar Dep. c. 91, ff. 187–190v.

36 Bloomfield's dispatch of 13 August 1865: PRO, FO 425/80.

37 Ibid.

38 Ibid.

39 Ibid.

addressed a letter to him,[40] declaring that *'le gouvernement impérial serait disposé à négocier un traité avec l'Angleterre.'* The basis of such a treaty should be the confidential draft which Lord Bloomfield had submitted on behalf of his government in June 1862, but which had not found favour with the Austrian Cabinet at that time (see above, pp. 22ff.). This meant that Austria would set an upper limit of approximately 15 per cent *ad valorem* (or an equivalent specific rate) to the duty leviable upon articles of British produce or manufacture. The reduction of the tariff would be gradual however; and the new rates would not become effective before 1 January 1867, but would be adopted no later than 1 January 1870. Only in the case of a few articles of British origin, such as plate glass, jute, and salt fish,[41] would the lower rates be introduced as early as 1 January 1867. At this date the high export duty on rags, whose reduction the British had been urging all along,[42] would be lowered by 50 per cent. For the rest, Austria would accord Britain most-favoured-nation treatment.

Given the strength of the protectionist forces in Austria, with whose opposition the government had to reckon, those were surprisingly liberal proposals. No wonder that Count Mensdorff insisted that his letter (whose substance he communicated to Bloomfield[43]) be treated as confidential, and that it must be considered as cancelled should the negotiations for the loan fail. As it was, the prospects of their succeeding seemed to be bright. 'I learn,' Earl Russell wrote to Bloomfield on 29 August 1865,[44] 'that the negotiations for a loan to the Austrian government, which is proposed to be contracted in this country through the medium

40 Enclosed in Bloomfield's dispatch of 13 August 1865: ibid.
41 British representations about the high rate of duty levied by Austria on imports of salt fish had been frequent; see above, pp. 27f. and 58.
42 See above, pp. 10, 15f., and 58.
43 Bloomfield's dispatch of 17 August 1865: PRO, FO 425/80. A few days later Mensdorff directed Count Apponyi, the Imperial ambassador to the Court of St James, officially to acquaint the British government with the Austrian offer (Instruction for Apponyi of 24 August 1865, trans. enclosed in Bloomfield's dispatch of 12 November 1865: ibid.). See also HHStA, Kabinettsarchiv, Ministerratsprotokolle, 10 November 1865.
44 PRO, FO 425/80.

of Mr. Somerset Beaumont, are progressing favourably.' Indeed, so optimistic was Earl Russell that he furnished Bloomfield with the draft of a treaty of commerce meant to serve as a basis for the impending negotiations with the Imperial government.[45] How much importance the Foreign Office attached to the business in hand was shown by its decision to dispatch Louis Mallet and Robert Morier to Vienna with instructions to assist the Ambassador in his negotiation.[46]

Meanwhile, on 2 September, Somerset Beaumont had returned to Vienna and informed the Austrian government that their application for a loan of £23 million had been favourably received by Baring and other capitalists in London, and that 'negotiations could be opened this week at Antwerp, after Mr. Baring had personally communicated with Mr. Hope of Amsterdam.'[47] About the same time a more formal proposition from Baring reached Count Larisch, the Minister of Finance, indicating 65 as the price at which the loan would be accepted, and requiring a 2 per cent commission on the whole amount. 'This proposition,' Lord Bloomfield reported to Earl Russell, 'has somewhat staggered the Austrian government, who had hoped for better terms; but they are nevertheless so desirous that the loan should be effected in England ... that they have resolved to go into the negotiation and to send M. Becke of the Finance Department to meet Messrs. Baring and Hope at Antwerp.'[48]

Becke's mission, however, was unsuccessful. Baring failed to secure Hope's cooperation, who took a dim view of Austria's financial situation and raised doubts about the constitutional power of the Imperial government to float a loan without obtaining the sanction of the *Reichsrat*. Thus, as Bloomfield's dispatch of 14 September 1865 stated, 'unless Messrs. Baring can come

45 Instruction for Bloomfield of 6 September 1865 with enclosure: ibid. On 14 September Bloomfield handed over a copy of this draft to Baron Meysenbug, the Acting Minister of Foreign Affairs (Bloomfield's dispatch of 14 September 1865: ibid.).
46 Instruction for Bloomfield of 7 September 1865: ibid.
47 Bloomfield's dispatch of 5 September 1865: ibid.
48 Ibid.

to some understanding with Messrs. Rothschild the affair will probably fall to the ground.'[49] As was to be expected, the Imperial government, threatened with failure to obtain a loan in the London money market, at once gave signs of having lost interest in the proposed Anglo-Austrian treaty of commerce. 'I regret to say,' Bloomfield reported to London, 'that the Austrian government feel less confident than they did ten days ago in their means of carrying out their commercial policy,' and he added that a high official in the Ministry of Foreign Affairs 'spoke with regret of the state of the negotiations for the loan and of the general unpopularity of Free Trade principles in Austria.'[50]

This disconcerting news evoked a spirited reply from Russell. 'I have to instruct you,' he wrote to Bloomfield, 'to urge on the Austrian government that the signature of a treaty of commerce with this country will facilitate the loan contemplated by that government. The Austrian government will do well in adopting a bold and decided policy in dealing with these matters.'[51] Since their hopes of placing a loan in London had faded anyway the Austrian government might have shrugged off Russell's implied warning. But Becke, who after Baring's negative response had proceeded to Paris where he was trying to get Baron James Rothschild interested in the projected loan, informed his superiors that this financial magnate also laid much weight on the conclusion of an Anglo-Austrian treaty of commerce.[52] In these circumstances the Imperial government could hardly venture to withdraw their offer of 12 August. To renege on their proposal to start negotiating a treaty of commerce would have been all the less advisable for the Austrians since this would have deprived them of their main argument against reconvening the Joint Commission of Inquiry – something they were obviously very anxious to avoid.[53]

49 Ibid. See also Steefel. p. 28 and Gille, II, 442.
50 Bloomfield's second dispatch of 14 September 1865: PRO, FO 425/80.
51 Instruction for Bloomfield of 21 September 1865: ibid. Earl Russell repeated this argument in his instruction for Bloomfield of 3 October 1865: ibid.
52 Steefel, p. 29.
53 In his talks with Bloomfield Count Mensdorff had stressed that, since Austria

Thus, rather than simply refuse to negotiate the Imperial government resorted to delaying tactics. Reasons – valid or pretended – for postponing the start of negotiations were easily found: Becke's absence from Vienna,[54] the long delay in the appointment of a Minister of Commerce,[55] a serious illness of Countess Mensdorff.[56] Faced with evasions of one kind or another, London at last could not help suspecting that Austria's 'apparent readiness to make a commercial treaty with Great Britain [was] only used as a means of obtaining a loan in London and Paris';[57] and Lord Bloomfield was authorized to threaten Vienna with the recall of Mallet and Morier.[58] As a matter of fact, the Ambassador had already hinted at such a possibility in his earlier conversations with Baron Meysenbug, the Acting Minister of Foreign Affairs, and had warned him that the departure of the two British experts, 'indicating as it would the suspension of the negotiations, would not only create a very bad impression on Her Majesty's government and on the public of England, but would certainly exercize the most prejudicial effect on the pending negotiations of the loan.'[59]

This time Bloomfield's energetic representations seemed to

---

was prepared to conclude a treaty of commerce, 'he saw no necessity for the re-assembling of the Commission'; his government, he added, 'objected to the important character which it had assumed' (Bloomfield's dispatch of 17 August 1865: PRO, FO 425/80). Three weeks later the Austrian Chargé d'Affaires in London told Russell that 'the Imperial government [were] desirous that the International Commission appointed in the early part of this year for the examination of the Austrian tariff ... should not assemble again; that the Imperial government [were] ready without further inquiries to conclude a treaty of commerce ... and that they consider[ed] this course preferable to the renewed sitting of the Commission.' (Instruction for Bloomfield of 6 September 1865: ibid.)

54 Bloomfield's dispatch of 21 September 1865: ibid.
55 Bloomfield's dispatches of 28 September and 18 October 1865: ibid.
56 Bloomfield's dispatch of 26 October 1865: ibid.
57 Instruction for Bloomfield of 10 October 1865: ibid.
58 Ibid. See also Bloomfield's dispatches of 18 and 19 October 1865 and the instruction sent to him on 23 October 1865: ibid.
59 Bloomfield's dispatch of 9 October 1865: ibid.

produce results. On 23 October the Council of Ministers, having been urged by Count Mensdorff to come to a decision, agreed to enter into formal negotiations with the British representatives.[60] Though the Austrian Cabinet need not at that moment have felt inhibited by fear of adverse parliamentary reactions to their decision – the constitution having recently been suspended – most of the Ministers seem to have given their consent only reluctantly. In the debate preceding the vote Baron Wüllerstorf, the recently appointed Minister of Commerce, deplored in no uncertain terms Mensdorff's rashness in having led the British government to expect that Austria would set an upper limit of 15 per cent *ad valorem* to her import duties. The most that could be conceded under the present circumstances, he declared, was a maximum rate of 25 per cent; further reductions might be introduced, but only gradually, over a period of several years.[61]

It was obvious that the man who, in his capacity as Minister of Commerce, was about to take charge of the Anglo-Austrian negotiations did not feel bound by an offer that had been made before he joined the Cabinet, and one which he regarded as much too open-handed. Indeed Wüllerstorf at once occupied himself with the drawing up of counter-proposals to the British draft treaty, whose main provisions had been based on that very offer.[62] In an informal interview with the British Ambassador Baron Wüllerstorf revealed what he had in mind. He intended, he said, 'to propose to [Britain] one of two alternatives – either to take 15 per cent as the maximum of duties to be levied on the importation into Austria of the produce and manufacture of the British dominions, with a long list of articles to which this amount of reduction could not be applied, or to take 25 per cent as the maximum duty without exception.'[63] Earl Russell, having been informed by Bloomfield of Wüllerstorf's intentions, at once consulted Gladstone, who, rather than risk wrecking the negotiations

60 HHStA, Kabinettsarchiv, Ministerratsprotokolle, 23 October 1865.
61 Ibid.
62 Mensdorff's letter to Bloomfield of 24 October 1865 (trans.), enclosed in Bloomfield's first dispatch of 26 October 1865: PRO, FO 425/80.
63 Bloomfield's second dispatch of 26 October 1865: ibid.

by a downright rejection of the Austrian proposals, opted for the second alternative. Bloomfield was instructed accordingly, but was enjoined to endeavour to obtain a promise that the maximum of 25 per cent would be lowered within a specified period of time.[64]

Thus the stage was set for formal negotiations. They opened in the Imperial Chancellery of State on 1 November. Lord Bloomfield, assisted by Mallet and Morier, represented Britain; Count Mensdorff and Baron Wüllerstorf were the Austrian plenipotentiaries. The latter at that first meeting read out a memorandum setting forth the modifications Austria wished to introduce into the project of a commercial treaty which Bloomfield had submitted on 14 September.[65] The proposed alterations were fairly numerous, but only two or three of them were of such a nature as to meet with serious British objections. One concerned the periods which the Austrians envisaged for the gradual reduction of their duties. These periods, Bloomfield felt, extended over altogether too many years: for instance, the date at which a maximum rate of 20 per cent *ad valorem* (or corresponding specific duties) would become operative might be as late as 1874. The British negotiators also expressed keen dissatisfaction with the meagre reduction of the export duty on rags which Austria was prepared to concede. 'If this were the only reduction made,' Morier observed, 'the rag trade with England would probably remain just where it was.'[66] No less contentious was Austria's demand that the British government should undertake to obtain from Parliament not only the abolition of the duties on timber – something they had spontaneously offered to do[67] – but also a reduction of the duties on wine and spirits.

Nevertheless, given an earnest desire on both sides to reach an understanding, even these material disagreements might have been resolved. Indeed a second meeting of the negotiators which took place on 4 November at the Ministry of Commerce seems

64 Instruction for Bloomfield of 31 October 1865: ibid.
65 Bloomfield's dispatch of 2 November 1865 with enclosure: ibid.
66 Morier's report of the proceedings at a conference held on 4 November, enclosed in Bloomfield's dispatch of 9 November 1865: ibid.
67 Instruction for Bloomfield of 18 September 1865: ibid.

to have passed off so satisfactorily that Lord Bloomfield afterwards remarked to Baron Wüllerstorf that he thought they had
got over their main difficulties. The latter, too, appeared optimistic: in reply to Bloomfield's question he expressed his hope that
the treaty would be signed in a fortnight.[68]

Very soon, however, following a meeting between Mallet and
Morier and a panel of Austrian civil servants, Bloomfield's confidence gave way to disappointment. The Austrian bureaucracy,
particularly one Herr de Pretis,[69] who represented the Ministry
of Commerce, seemed to be much more intransigent than their
Ministers. This is how Robert Morier described the atmosphere
of that conference of experts.

M. de Pretis ... took into his hands the entire management of the discussion, only occasionally referring to Baron Gagern for a confirmation
of his statements; and it should be observed that both in his manner
and in his mode of expression this gentleman presented a remarkable
contrast to any of the Austrian officials with whom, up to the present
time, the English negotiators have had to deal. In lieu of generalities
and ambiguous phrases, combined with studied and artificial courtesy,
M. de Pretis displayed a thorough professional knowledge of his subject;
proved that he had a firm grasp of the worst errors of protection, of
which, though he would repudiate the charge, he is an intelligent disciple;
and evinced by his manner that he considered he was dealing with persons
who were desirous to overreach him, and therefore to be treated with
the minimum of civility necessary to render intercourse possible. It was
clear that we had at last penetrated to the real elements with which
we had to deal, and, moreover, that M. de Pretis was standing upon
different ground from that hitherto occupied by the Austrian negotiators.
It is further worthy of remark that he invariably spoke in the first person:
'*Je ne veux pas concéder ceci*'; '*Ne vous imaginez pas que vous obtien-
drez cela de moi*'; and the like.[70]

68 Bloomfield's dispatch of 9 November 1865: ibid.
69 Sisinio de Pretis, created Baron de Pretis von Cagnodo in 1870, later served
as Minister of Commerce and Minister of Finance respectively in three Austrian
Cabinets.
70 Morier's report of the proceedings at a conference held on 6 November,
enclosed in Bloomfield's dispatch of 9 November 1865: PRO, FO 425/80.

The British negotiators might have put up with de Pretis's churlish and overweening manners; what was more alarming from their point of view was that he suddenly raised demands which far exceeded those previously advanced by Baron Wüllerstorf. The British government, he insisted, should engage 'to recommend to Parliament the abolition of the duties on the importation of wood, timber and corn' and 'the reduction of the duties on the importation of wine, beer, meal, tobacco and beetroot sugar.'[71] It was impossible for the Austrian government, de Pretis argued, to sign a treaty which would not contain on the face of it counter-concessions and what he called tariff equivalents: the abolition of the timber duties could not be regarded as a sufficient equivalent for the concessions Austria was prepared to make.

Not unnaturally the two British experts refused even to discuss these new demands. Equivalents and 'fiscal' duties, Mallet reminded de Pretis, were matters that had been 'from the very earliest stages of the negotiation' and 'with the full and perfect knowledge of the Austrian government' excluded from consideration.[72]

Two days after this abortive conference Mallet, acting on Bloomfield's orders, called on Baron Wüllerstorf with a view to finding out whether de Pretis's extravagant demands had his backing. It became apparent at once that the Minister had indeed shifted his ground. 'He must,' he said, 'have something to show to the public in return for the large reductions in the Austrian tariff which he proposed to make.' The repeal of the timber duties was not enough. 'Unless some additional concession could be found ... he could not undertake the responsibility of concluding the treaty; and if the Imperial government insisted upon it, he should request the Emperor to accept his resignation.'[73]

This was an oblique admission that there existed differences of opinion within the Austrian Cabinet. Yet almost in the same

---

71 Ibid.
72 Ibid.
73 Mallet's report on his interview with Wüllerstorf, enclosed in Bloomfield's dispatch of 9 November 1865: ibid.

breath Wüllerstorf assured Mallet that even Mensdorff, the Minister of Foreign Affairs, accepted the proposition that 'it was essential to the conclusion of the treaty that some concessions should be made by England in respect of some at least of the Austrian products now taxed (and some of them heavily taxed) in the United Kingdom.'[74] There can be no doubt, however, that Mensdorff did not wish to risk a rupture of the Anglo-Austrian negotiation. Having been cautioned by Bloomfield that such would be unavoidable if the Imperial government insisted on Wüllerstorf's conditions,[75] he pleaded with his ministerial colleagues not to let that happen. A rupture of the negotiation, he told them, would be 'very harmful, not so much on account of the loan as on political grounds.'[76]

The Council of Ministers had to pay some heed to Mensdorff's warning; but the minutes of the meeting make it very clear that all the Cabinet was really interested in was 'to pacify England, so as to gain time for entering into negotiations with France.'[77] Hence it was decided to offer Britain a 'preliminary treaty,' one that would leave all or most of the controversial issues in abeyance. As will be seen presently this was the basis on which the two parties finally reached an agreement.

Meanwhile Lord Bloomfield decided to send Morier to London so that the Cabinet could receive an exact and detailed account of the state of affairs at Vienna.[78] The sudden departure of one

---

74 Ibid.
75 Bloomfield's dispatch of 9 November 1865: ibid.
76 HHStA, Kabinettsarchiv, Ministerratsprotokolle, 10 November 1865. Mensdorff must have known that Count Larisch, the Minister of Finance, had that very day instructed his representative in Paris to break off negotiations with James Rothschild, and to sign a loan contract with a rival syndicate of financiers (see Steefel, pp. 34ff.). Therefore the success of Austria's attempt to obtain a foreign loan no longer depended on a favourable outcome of her commercial negotiation with Britain, as it might have done had Baring and the London house of Rothschild still been among the prospective lenders (see above, p. 67).
77 HHStA, Kabinettsarchiv, Ministerratsprotokolle, 10 November 1865 (trans.): ibid.
78 Bloomfield's dispatch of 13 November 1865: PRO, FO 425/80.

of Bloomfield's technical advisers and the simultaneous decampment of Somerset Beaumont created a sensation in Vienna. The press not unnaturally considered these moves symptomatic of a rupture of the negotiations; but the prospect of an Anglo-Austrian treaty of commerce had been so unpopular that the newspapers, so far from taking alarm at the supposed turn of events, 'one and all ... hail[ed] it with satisfaction.'[79] The Imperial government, obviously embarrassed, hastened to issue a semi-official denial that there was any question of the negotiation's being broken off. Yet in point of fact it was on the verge of collapse.

Morier reached London on 17 November.[80] His oral report, as well as the contents of two dispatches from Bloomfield which he had brought along were so discouraging that the Earl of Clarendon (who had recently succeeded Russell at the Foreign Office) concluded that it was 'hopeless to expect a favourable result from negotiations conducted in such a spirit on the part of Austria. ... It only remains, therefore, for Her Majesty's government to declare that, the negotiations having been virtually broken off by the Austrian government, ... Her Majesty's government hold the negotiations to be now entirely at an end.'[81]

This, however, was not Clarendon's last word. He may have encountered opposition to his uncompromising stand among some members of the Cabinet, or he may, as he averred in a subsequent instruction for Bloomfield,[82] have been slightly encouraged by the Ambassador's most recent dispatches, which contained some evidence of the Austrians' desire to avoid a rupture of the negotiation. Whatever his reasons, the Foreign Secretary did revoke, albeit in an oblique manner, his dispatch of 17 November. Indeed he authorized Bloomfield to assure Vienna that 'Her Majesty's government are animated by a sincere desire to avert, if possible, from Austria the embarrassment, political as well as financial, which would ensue from the negotiation being brought abruptly to a close.'[83] Indicative of the Cabinet's conciliatory attitude was

79 Bloomfield's dispatch of 16 November 1865: ibid.
80 Instruction for Bloomfield of 17 November 1865: ibid.
81 Ibid.
82 Instruction for Bloomfield of 20 November 1865: ibid.
83 Ibid.

an offer by Gladstone to concede a demand which the Austrians had urged all along. It concerned the reduction of the high duty on Hungarian wines imported in bottles. After his arrival in London Robert Morier had laid this matter before the Chancellor of the Exchequer, who authorized him to state on his return to Vienna 'that, if the Austrian government could adduce satisfactory proof that the reduction of the duty on wine in bottles to the rate paid by wine in wood would enable low-priced Austrian wines to obtain access to the British market, from which they are now excluded or to which they have but a limited and difficult access, and that by reason of the restriction thus removed this branch of commerce would derive a benefit which might fairly warrant the loss of revenue caused by the reduction, then Her Majesty's government would be ready to accede to the wishes of the Austrian government.'[84]

While making these fresh overtures to Vienna the British government were determined, however, to leave the Austrians in no doubt that their patience was exhausted, and that any further vacillation or procrastination would spell the end of the negotiation. Thus before sending Morier back to Vienna Lord Clarendon summoned Count Wimpffen, the Austrian Chargé d'Affaires, and delivered what, for all its polite form, was in substance an ultimatum. He asked him to inform his government

qu'à son plus grand regret il doit considérer rupture des négociations commerciales comme inévitable; qu'en aucun cas il n'en veut continuer les négociations qui, en se prolongeant, ne pourraient qu'apporter de l'aigreur dans nos bons rapports auxquels il attache le plus grand prix; mais que, si dans le courant de la semaine prochaine le gouvernement Impérial lui fournissait le moyen par des propositions acceptables de pouvoir s'entendre et de *conclure* [Wimpffen's italics], il saisissait cette possibilité à deux mains.[85]

The Austrian government could not mistake the meaning of

84 Notes of the proceedings at a meeting held at the Austrian Chancellery of State on 27 November 1865, enclosed in Bloomfield's dispatch of 30 November 1865: ibid.

85 Count Wimpffen's telegraphic dispatch of 19 November 1865: HHStA, Administrative Registratur, F34, Sonderreihe, Karton 32, r2, 1 Varia.

this message; and for once Mensdorff's conciliatory point of view seems to have carried the day. Within three days of Wimpffen's telegram the Council of Ministers met and gave its approval to a draft of a commercial treaty which, though it still contained two articles to which the British were sure to object, was clearly intended to form the basis of an understanding.[86] As a matter of fact, Bloomfield, who had been furnished with a copy of the Austrian draft immediately after the meeting of the Council, took a favourable view of its provisions. 'Although it does not contain all that can be desired,' he wrote to Earl Clarendon, 'there is much in it which would prove advantageous to the interests of Her Majesty's subjects, and as such I do not hesitate to submit it to your Lordship's consideration.'[87] In a conversation with Mensdorff, however, the Ambassador felt obliged to express his disappointment with Article VI of the document, which provided only for a trifling reduction of the Austrian export duty on rags and made no mention at all of the promised downward revision of the duties on herring, jute, and plate glass. He also took exception to Article VII, which, albeit in a very vague form, still referred to 'concessions on the part of England.'[88]

But having voiced these objections, Bloomfield at once suggested – as his 'private opinion, entirely unauthorized by Her Majesty's government' – a way of getting round these last major stumbling blocks. Why should not Articles VI and VII be omitted from the treaty altogether? Instead any mutual concessions could form the subject of an exchange of notes or of a protocol in which the two governments would pledge themselves to carry out certain tariff reductions in the way of autonomous legislative enactment.[89] Having previously assured himself of Wüllerstorf's assent to this proposal,[90] Lord Bloomfield presented it formally during a conference held at the Chancellery of State on 27 Novem-

86 HHStA, Kabinettsarchiv, Ministerratsprotokolle, 22 November 1865.
87 Bloomfield's dispatch of 23 November 1865: PRO, FO 425/80.
88 Ibid.
89 Ibid.
90 Bloomfield's dispatch of 26 November 1865: ibid.

ber 1865, and obtained its acceptance by the Austrian delegates.[91]

Now, at long last, the way was open to an agreement. A few technical details having been cleared up to mutual satisfaction, Lord Bloomfield on 1 December forwarded to London a translation of the German text of the treaty as finally agreed to by the Austrian plenipotentiaries and himself.[92] He expressed his 'confident belief that [the draft] will be found substantially to secure the objects sought by Her Majesty's government in entering upon the negotiation,' and added the warning that, 'unless any alterations ... appear essential to Her Majesty's government, the suggestion of further changes might give occasion to delay and difficulty in bringing the negotiation to a close.'[93] The Ambassador's hopes were not disappointed: his government very quickly approved of the draft and authorized him to sign the treaty without delay.[94]

Yet before the plenipotentiaries finally affixed their signatures and seals to the instrument there arose some last-minute wrangles, not indeed about the stipulations of the treaty, but about those of the protocol that was to accompany it. Bloomfield tried once more to persuade the Austrians to agree to a more substantial reduction of their export duty on rags than they had offered.[95] But all he was able to obtain was a lowering, long since promised, of the import duty on salted herring.[96] The Austrians did not gain all their ends either; but at the last moment they managed to carry one point that was of considerable importance to them.

91 Bloomfield's telegraphic dispatch of 27 November 1865 and Morier's notes of the proceedings at the conference, enclosed in Bloomfield's dispatch of 30 November 1865: ibid.
92 Bloomfield's dispatch of 1 December 1865 with enclosure: ibid.
93 Ibid.
94 Clarendon's telegram to Bloomfield of 6 December, followed by detailed instructions of 7 December 1865: ibid. The English version of the draft which Bloomfield had submitted was slightly revised by London; but the alterations were merely 'intended to make the language more conformable to the English idiom.'
95 Bloomfield's telegraphic dispatch of 13 December 1865: ibid. See also Clarendon's instruction no. 17 of 7 December 1865: ibid.
96 Article v of the Final Protocol: *British and Foreign State Papers 1864–1865*, LV, 15f.

They argued, not without reason, that Gladstone's offer to lower the import duty on bottled wines (see above, p. 75) was too hedged in to be of much value; and they insisted that Britain should give an *unconditional* undertaking to carry out that reduction.[97] This point of view was strongly supported by Bloomfield, and on 13 December he was authorized by his government to accede to the Austrian demand and to have the concession recorded in the Final Protocol.[98]

Three days later, in the afternoon of 16 December 1865, the Anglo-Austrian treaty of commerce, first mooted in July 1860 by Count Rechberg (see above, p. 13), was signed;[99] the ratifications were exchanged at the Imperial Chancellery of State on 4 January 1866.[100] The British negotiators and their government were elated. 'The triumph is complete,' Robert Morier wrote to his father on 21 December. 'They are much pleased at home and we, Mallet and I, have had a very *splendissime* despatch, praising us for the ability and all manner of fine things with which we have worked out the good work.'[101] As a recognition of their services both Morier and Mallet received the Companionship of the Bath. In the case of the former the distinction was one which had never before been conferred on a person of his official rank.[102]

London seemed to have every reason to be pleased with the outcome of the negotiation. When all was said and done Britain had made only a few minor concessions. Her undertaking to extend to Austria the same commercial advantages which she had conceded to the French under the Cobden Treaty merely

97 Bloomfield's second dispatch of 1 December 1865: PRO, FO 425/80.
98 Clarendon's telegram to Bloomfield of 13 December 1865: ibid.
99 Bloomfield s telegraphic dispatch of 16 December 1865: ibid. Somerset Beaumont, anxious as always to obtain official status, had begged Lord Clarendon to reward his 'sacrifices and exertions' by authorizing him to add his signature to that of Lord Bloomfield on the treaty; he had even enlisted Count Mensdorff in support of his request. The would-be diplomat was bitterly disappointed when the Foreign Secretary refused to humour his vanity. See Beaumont's letters to Carendon of 10 November and 18 December 1865: Bodleian Library, M.S. Clar Dep. C. 91. ff. 198–202.
100 Bloomfield's telegraphic dispatch of 4 January 1866: PRO, FO 425/80.
101 Wemyss, II, 17.
102 Ibid.

gave conventional sanction to the existing state of affairs (see above p. 9f.). As for the abolition of the timber duties and the reduction of the duties on wine in bottles, these hardly involved any heavy fiscal sacrifices.[103]

Austria, on the other hand, under Article III of the treaty had yielded to Britain's main demand. She had bound herself to revise her customs tariff in such a way that from 1 January 1867 the import duties levied on British commodities would not exceed 25 per cent of their value (including the cost of transport, insurance, and commission), and that from 1 January 1870 the maximum of these duties would be set at 20 per cent of the value (with the additions above defined).

The meaning of this crucial article would have been unambiguous, and its implementation would have presented no difficulty had Austria been prepared to abandon her primitive method of calculating customs duties by weight in favour of an *ad valorem* system. However such a reform (which would not only have presupposed a more highly trained body of customs officers than Austria possessed, but might have seriously weakened the protective function of her tariff in case foreign prices were lowered) was out of the question, and the British, who had at first suggested it,[104] did not insist.[105] Indeed they consented to the insertion in the treaty of a clause which explicitly provided for the maintenance by Austria of 'the present system of calculating customs duties by weight' (Article III). But how, given this system of 'specific' duties by weight, were the stipulated maximum *ad val-*

---

103 Lord Bloomfield estimated the loss of revenue occasioned by the reduction of the wine duties at £80,000. (See the notes of meetings and conferences held between the British and Austrian negotiators during the week ended 16 December 1865, enclosed in Bloomfield's dispatch of 19 December 1865: PRO, FO 425/80.) The total loss of revenue was later stated by Bloomfield and Mallet to have amounted to £392,000. (See their note to Baron Beust of 4 May 1868, enclosed in Bloomfield's note to Lord Stanley of the same date: PRO, FO 425/91.)
104 Bonar's dispatch of 4 March 1865: PRO, FO 425/79.
105 See the copy of William Hutt's private letter to Baron Gagern of — June 1865, enclosed in the former's dispatch to Earl Russell of 27 June 1865: PRO, FO 425/80.

orem rates of Article III to be ascertained and put in operation? An answer to this question was given in Article IV of the treaty and in an explanatory article of the Final Protocol. The former reads as follows:[106]

Commissioners from both governments shall meet not later than the month of March 1866, for the purpose of ascertaining and determining the values and additional charges [referred to in Article III], and they shall take as the basis of their calculations the average prices at the principal centres of production and commerce of the United Kingdom for the year 1865.

The principles that were to govern the work of those commissioners were more clearly defined in Article II of the Final Protocol.[107]

In order to avoid any future doubt as to the intention of Article III [of the treaty] the plenipotentiaries of the two Powers agreed to the following explanation:
     In the construction of a tariff of specific duties by weight within fixed *ad valorem* rates, it is necessary to determine what shall be the unit of value to which each specific duty shall be applied.
     In adopting the basis of value established by Article III it is understood that it is not intended to depart from the general principle of the Article, viz., the application of certain maximum *ad valorem* rates of duty to all articles of British produce and manufacture, but to guard against the necessity of making separate provision for every variety of each article, thereby creating minute and inconvenient subdivisions in the tariff.[108]

106 *Bri.. sh and Foreign State Papers, 1864–1865*, LV, 9.
107 Ibid., pp. 13f.
108 In a conference of experts held on 12 December 1865 in the Ministry of Commerce Louis Mallet himself rejected 'a minute and elaborate specific system which should record a separate duty for every imaginable article,' on the ground that 'there was nothing British commerce had so great a horror of as a complicated and minutely subdivided tariff.' See the notes of meetings and conferences enclosed in Bloomfield's dispatch of 19 December 1865: PRO, FO 425/80.

With this in view it becomes necessary to group together those different qualities and descriptions of the same article or of similar articles which, from their approximation in value and general resemblance in character, it is found possible to include under one and the same denomination in one position of the tariff.

But it is understood that in fixing the denominations in each position of the future Austrian tariff they shall be so arranged that the duty affixed to any one position shall not exceed the 'maximum' rates fixed by Article III of the treaty upon the average value of any kind of goods of commercial importance included under any one denomination in such a position, unless by common consent it is considered expedient or necessary.

In contrast to these detailed and highly technical stipulations Article v of the treaty is short and, as Mallet admitted, it was 'worded somewhat vaguely with a deliberate intention of avoiding criticism on the part of the Austrian public and of assisting the Austrian government in their negotiations with France.'[109] Like the two articles which preceded it, this one also left some very important matters to be settled at a future date. 'Those duties of the future Austrian tariff,' it reads, 'to come into operation on the 1st of January, 1867, to which England attaches a special interest, shall form the subject of a supplementary Convention to be concluded between the two contracting parties.'[110]

Hence it was not a slip of the pen when Louis Mallet in a detailed analysis of the instrument which he had helped to draw up spoke of it as 'this preliminary treaty.'[111] Before long Britain was to find out that for all its careful preparation the Convention of 16 December 1865 was indeed little more than a *pactum de paciscendo*. What is more, for five years to come Austria even evaded her contractual obligation to 'covenant.'

109 Mallet's report to Bloomfield of 1 December 1865, enclosed in the latter's dispatch of the same date: ibid.
110 *British and Foreign State Papers, 1864–1865,* LV, 10.
111 Mallet's report as quoted above, in n. 109.

5
Protocols

The reader who may have secretly blamed himself for his failure to fathom the exact meaning of Articles III and IV of the December treaty – not to speak of the abstruse 'explanatory' clauses of the Final Protocol which were supposed to clarify them – may derive some comfort from the fact that the very men who had agreed upon their wording soon afterwards found it possible to quarrel about their proper interpretation. As will be seen presently the purport of those articles – the question of how to 'translate' the *ad valorem* 'maxima' rates prescribed by Article III of the treaty into the form of specific duties by weight – became the subject of long and frustrating arguments between the Austrian and the British diplomats.

But if the interpretation of those intricate stipulations could give rise to legalistic disputes, there was no room for quibbles regarding the dates fixed by the treaty: the first reduction of the Austrian duties levied upon British imports was to take place on 1 January 1867; and a Mixed Commission which would have to ascertain, as a necessary preliminary to that step, the average prices of British articles imported into Austria was to meet 'not later than the month of March, 1866' (Article IV). Yet one wonders whether the Austrians had ever intended to meet these deadlines. The ink of their signatures to the treaty was hardly dry before they began to plead with the British government for a deferment. To start with, the Imperial government requested and obtained

London's consent to have the first meeting of the commissioners postponed till May, 1866.[1] By then, however, the Austrians, preoccupied with vital matters of state – the impending clash of arms with Prussia and her Italian ally – were even less likely to concern themselves with the implementation of the December treaty; and once war had broken out they could argue plausibly that tariff negotiations must await more tranquil times. London could not well refuse to accept this plea; and by a protocol signed in Vienna by the British and Austrian representatives on 2 July 1866 it was agreed to adjourn until three months after the conclusion of peace the commission appointed in virtue of Article IV of the December treaty.

The military conflict between Austria and Prussia was decided more quickly than anyone could have foreseen. On 3 July, less than two weeks after the Prussian troops had crossed the Bohemian borders, they inflicted a crushing defeat on Austria's northern army at Sadowa (Königgrätz). Soon afterwards an armistice was arranged and the treaty of Prague, signed on 23 August 1866, formally ended the state of hostilities between the Habsburg monarchy and Prussia. It took only a little longer to settle affairs in the southern theatre of war: a treaty which restored peace between the Kingdom of Italy and Austria was concluded at Vienna on 3 October 1866. Thus the Anglo-Austrian tariff commission, which, by the protocol of 2 July, had been adjourned until three months after the end of the war, would have to reassemble and resume its labours at the latest some time in January 1867.

When, early in November, the British Chargé d'Affaires reminded Baron Wüllerstorf of this deadline, the Minister assured him that he was 'willing scrupulously to abide by his former engagement,' though he had 'conceived a hope that a further short delay might be allowed to him.'[2] What was merely a *ballon d'essai* at that moment a few weeks later assumed the form of

1 The diplomatic correspondence pertaining to the postponement of the Anglo-Austrian commission is missing both in the PRO and the HHStA. However references in later documents, especially the retrospective account contained in Bloomfield's and Mallet's note to Baron Beust of 4 May 1868 (PRO, FO 425/91), make it possible to reconstruct the sequence of events.
2 Bonar's dispatch of 6 November 1866: PRO, FO 425/88.

an official request, when Baron Beust, who had in the meantime
succeeded Count Mensdorff as Minister of Foreign Affairs, proposed to the British government to postpone the commencement
of the commercial negotiations until 1 March 1867.[3]

Beust's main argument in support of his request was that by
Article XIII of the Treaty of Prague Austria was under the necessity
of negotiating a revision of her commercial treaty with the German
Customs Union. These negotiations were about to open at Vienna.
But if the Habsburg monarchy were to grant tariff concessions
to Britain before coming to terms with Prussia she would lose
all her trump cards: for, by virtue of the most-favoured-nation
clause in her existing treaty with the *Zollverein*, any benefits
accorded to a third Power would automatically accrue to Prussia
and her German associates. Surely, Beust pleaded, London would
not wish to see Austria's bargaining power thus weakened, seeing
that by Article VII of the December treaty British subjects would
share whatever commercial advantages Vienna might be able to
extract from Prussia.

Lord Stanley, the Foreign Secretary in the third Derby-Disraeli
Ministry, which had taken office the previous June, after consulting the Lords of Trade accepted Beust's arguments, and directed
the British Chargé d'Affaires to inform the Austrian Minister that
'Her Majesty's government [were] prepared to accede to [his]
request,' on the understanding that the new date for the resumption of the sitting of the Mixed Commission be recorded in the
form of a protocol.[4] Such a document was executed by Beust
and Bonar on 8 February 1867,[5] but not before the latter had
found it necessary to ward off an attempt by the wily Austrians
to insinuate into its text a clause implying that under certain
circumstances Britain might altogether renounce her right to a
commission as stipulated by Article IV of the December treaty.[6]

Nor was this abortive manoeuvre, which, as Lord Stanley

3 Beust's note to Bonar of 24 December 1866, enclosed in the latter's dispatch
of 25 December 1866: ibid.
4 Lord Stanley's instruction for Bonar of 8 January 1867: ibid.
5 Enclosed in Bonar's dispatch of 8 February 1867: ibid.
6 See Bonar's dispatch of 20 January 1867, with enclosure, and Stanley's instruction for Bonar of 26 January 1867: PRO, FO 425/89.

pointed out,[7] had produced a very unfavourable impression in London, the only indication of renewed efforts on the part of Austria to evade her obligation, or at least to delay its discharge. On the very day when Beust signed the Protocol by which he engaged to open the sitting of the Mixed Commission on 1 March 1867 Count Apponyi called upon Lord Stanley and informed him that his government, while 'ready to resume the negotiations according to promise, ... felt bound in fairness to state their opinion that it is not likely that anything of real importance could be accomplished until the negotiations now in progress [with] Italy and the *Zollverein* are concluded.'[8] The latter, however, as Lord Stanley knew, had just ended in disagreement and been adjourned indefinitely. (The new treaty of commerce between Austria and the German Customs Union was to be concluded only on 9 March 1868.)

The breakdown in the negotiations with Prussia and the departure for Florence of M. de Pretis – 'the only person whom the Imperial government would willingly appoint to confer with the British commissioners'[9] – served as a pretext for yet another Austrian request for a postponement of the commission. Bonar, an old hand at the diplomatic game with the Austrians, offered Lord Stanley a realistic if cheerless assessment of the situation:

It is hardly to be supposed that [Austria] would now allow the same advantages to accrue to the *Zollverein* indirectly, without any compensation soever, and solely through the negotiations ... with Great Britain, ... which but a week ago she so peremptorily refused to the Prussian commissioners ... She will consider herself now compelled ... to postpone all further or notable modification of her tariff in favour of other countries until after some understanding shall have been arrived with the *Zollverein*. Under these circumstances, what would be the present prospects of the British commissioners at Vienna? Whatever their powers of persuasion or the prospective advantages to her commerce which might be held out to Austria, I have reason to believe that the latter would not

7 Instruction for Lord Bloomfield of 20 February 1867: ibid.
8 Mr Egerton of the Foreign Office to Mr Farrer of the Board of Trade: 9 February 1867: ibid. See also the instruction for Bloomfield quoted in n. 7.
9 Bonar's dispatch of 12 February 1867: ibid.

now, under any circumstances, conclude a further treaty with Great Britain, save conditionally, that is to say, providing that its operation should be subject to the previous conclusion of her treaty with Prussia and the *Zollverein*.[10]

Referring next to the alleged difficulty created by the absence of M. de Pretis, whose return to Vienna was not expected before the middle of April, the Chargé d'Affaires concluded his sober account with the following recommendations. He, Bonar, or Lord Bloomfield should be authorized to 'go through the ceremony of opening the Commission *pro formâ* on the 1st of March, as stipulated in the Protocol signed ... on the 8th instant, but that the British commissioners should postpone their arrival at Vienna until they considered the circumstances more opportune.'[11]

Needless to say, Lord Stanley received the news from the Austrian capital with indignation. His first inclination, as he admitted to Lord Bloomfield,[12] was to send Mallet at once to Vienna with orders to insist on the strict fulfilment of the engagements Austria had undertaken. He soon realized, however, that while he could undoubtedly enforce compliance with the letter of the December treaty and the February Protocol, he had no means of compelling the Austrian government to negotiate in good faith. In this mood of frustration the Foreign Secretary may even, by implication, have placed some blame for the impasse on Bloomfield: he seems to have felt that the Austrians had taken advantage of the Ambassador's prolonged absence from Vienna. Be that as it may, Bloomfield received peremptory orders to return to his post without delay.[13] He arrived at Vienna on 26 February,[14] in good time for the farce which he, Beust, Wüllerstorf, and Gagern were to enact on 1 March, when they met in formal session to comply with the provisions of the February Protocol, but merely agreed to adjourn the Mixed Commission to 1 May 1867.[15] Yet another Protocol recording this decision was signed by Beust

10 Ibid.
11 Ibid.
12 Instruction for Bloomfield of 20 February 1867: ibid.
13 Ibid.
14 Bloomfield's dispatch of 1 March 1867: ibid.
15 Ibid.

and Bloomfield on 16 March,[16] less than a month later.

This latest postponement need not have mattered very greatly even from the British point of view, seeing that according to the Protocol of 2 July 1866 the reduced Austrian customs duties to be worked out by the Mixed Commission were to become operative at the latest eight months after its start. However, since the aforementioned meeting of 1 March 1867 was construed to signify the formal commencement of the negotiation, the new rates would have had to be introduced in any case on 1 January 1868. Referring to this date Baron Beust, in an attempt to reassure the British, made the following confident statement. '*Les six mois qui restent* [after 1 May] *jusqu'à l'expiration du terme de huit mois nous semblent suffire pour accomplir la tâche dévolue à cette Commission.*'[17] Had the Austrians been prepared to cooperate in earnest with their British colleagues on the Mixed Commission there would indeed have been ample time after 1 May to work out an agreement on the revision of the Austrian tariff. As it was, such a spirit of cooperation was totally lacking. From the very start the Austrians in their usual fashion resorted to dilatory tactics, legalistic argumentation, and pleas for 'understanding.'

There is no need to trace all the twists and turns of the new negotiation. Suffice it to say that the atmosphere in which it came to be conducted had not at all been improved by the resignation, in April 1867, of Baron Wüllerstorf and the appointment *ad interim* of Baron Becke as head of the Austrian Ministry of Commerce. The latter turned out to be much more intransigent, and certainly less polite, than his predecessor, who was credited by Bonar with being sincere in his aim 'to inaugurate in Austria a liberal commercial system.'[18] Mallet, who, together with Morier, had

16 Enclosed in Bloomfield's dispatch of 16 March 1867: ibid.
17 Memorandum read by Beust at the meeting on 1 March 1867, enclosed in Bloomfield's dispatch of the same date: ibid.
18 Bonar's dispatch of 12 November 1866: PRO, FO 425/88, no. 6. That Wüllerstorf was a liberal at heart is borne out by a memorandum of 22 June 1866 addressed to Mensdorff, which, though drafted by a senior official, was signed by the Minister and undoubtedly expressed his views correctly. This document is quoted *in extenso* by Adolf Beer, *Die österreichische Handelspolitik im neunzehnten Jahrhundert* (Vienna, 1891), pp. 374ff.

by that time taken charge of the negotiation on the British side, was shocked to hear the new man speak of the December convention 'in a very different tone from that which [he] had been accustomed to hear from Count Mensdorff and Baron Wüllerstorf,'[19] both of whom had never failed to stress their willingness faithfully to abide by the stipulations of that treaty. Becke, however, under heavy pressure from the Chambers of Commerce, frankly disavowed the possibility of the tariff reform to which Austria was committed by Article III of the treaty of commerce. 'He must beg me distinctly to understand,' Mallet quoted him as saying, 'that if I contemplated as a result of the present negotiation any changes in the Austrian tariff which would materially modify either the rates of duty or the principles upon which it is constructed, he did not hesitate to say that for his part it would be entirely out of his power at the present moment to agree thereon.'[20]

What survives of the internal correspondence of Imperial officials, for instance a memorandum of 16 June 1867, addressed to Baron Beust by M. de Pretis in the name of the Minister of Commerce,[21] provides further evidence to show that the Austrians had no intention of negotiating in good faith. The writer referred to Britain's failure to show understanding for Austria's reluctance to prejudice her impending negotiations with Prussia. This, he argued, left the Imperial government 'no other choice but to cling strictly to the letter of the [December] treaty, and to defend as far as possible the existing tariff positions' – in other words, to exploit to the full the opportunities for quibbling so happily afforded by the ambiguous wording of certain articles of the Treaty and the Final Protocol. Insistence by Austria on her own interpretation of these crucial articles, de Pretis predicted, would soon cause the Anglo-Austrian negotiation to take 'an unpleasant turn'; and he concluded by suggesting that 'it must be left to the British Cabinet whether, under these circumstances, they still feel bound to insist on the continuation of the negotiation.'

19 Mallet's report to Lord Stanley of 19 May 1867: PRO, FO 425/90.
20 Ibid.
21 HHStA, Administrative Registratur, F34, Sonderreihe, Karton 32, r2, 1 Varia, 1. Teil (trans.).

The tactics recommended by M. de Pretis came to be employed very effectively by the Austrian representatives on the Mixed Commission that was charged with establishing the values of British goods to which, when imported into Austria, the maximum duty of 25 per cent *ad valorem* was to be applied after 1 January 1868. This task, given Austria's refusal to change her system of calculating customs duties by weight, was not a simple one: to construct a tariff of specific duties by weight within fixed *ad valorem* rates might have resulted in the listing of thousands of individual items. Since such a minutely subdivided tariff was obviously impracticable, the Final Protocol of 1865, as has been shown, had provided for some method of averaging the prices 'of the same article or of similar articles which, from their approximation in value and general resemblance in character, it [would be] found possible to include under one and the same denomination.' It was over the application of this principle that serious dissensions arose between the British and the Austrian commissioners. The latter, in carrying out an assessment of average British prices, insisted on lumping together articles known commonly by one name (e.g., 'bleached cotton cloth') but of very different qualities and values, irrespective of the quantities in which these goods were produced or of their importance as articles of commerce. Such a procedure was, of course, altogether unacceptable to the British; for averages struck in this way would have meant that the cheaper, mass-produced goods of British make would have to pay a much higher import duty than 25 per cent. As Louis Mallet pointed out to the Austrian commissioners, 'the interpretation ... put upon the Treaty and the Final Protocol by [them] amounted to a change of the principle of the Treaty from a *maximum* rate of 25 per cent of the value to an *average* rate of 25 per cent, an interpretation which would render the whole intention of the treaty null and void.'[22] Over this fundamental issue the Mixed Commission became hopelessly deadlocked. The British representatives could no longer doubt that 'the object at which the Austrian commissioners were aiming was to gain as much time as possible in the hope of ... exhausting the patience

22 Mallet's report to Lord Stanley of 22 June 1867: PRO, FO 425/90.

of Her Majesty's government, so as to lead them to accept results which would fall far short of their legitimate treaty claims.'[23]

Meanwhile the Austrians had found yet another pretext for procrastination. In June 1867 the long-sought reconciliation between the Crown and the Hungarians, who for many years past had practised a policy of sullen abstention and passive resistance, was accomplished. A constitutional compromise, aimed at the reconstruction of the Habsburg monarchy along dualist lines, gave Hungary a large measure of autonomy and a voice equal to that of 'Austria'[24] in the common affairs of the Empire. In consequence of Hungary's new political status – as early as February she had acquired a government of her own – representatives of her Ministry of Commerce were appointed to the Mixed Commission.[25] These gentlemen, however, were in no hurry: they did not arrive at Vienna before the middle of June, thus causing further delays in the work of the commission, since its Austrian members refused to discuss the vital question of the iron duties in the absence of their Hungarian colleagues.[26] (One of the latter, Mallet found out, was personally interested in the iron works of Kaschau,[27] a fact which did not make him the most unbiased of experts.)

The adverse consequences of the constitutional reforms for the Anglo-Austrian negotiation were, however, much more serious than that. The new impediments (or what the Austrians gladly chose to represent as such) were first mentioned by Baron Gagern

23 Mallet's report to Lord Stanley of 25 June 1867: ibid.
24 After 1867 the non-Hungarian half of the Habsburg State came to be known officially as 'the Kingdoms and Lands represented in the *Reichsrat*.' In common parlance, however, this cumbrous term was never used, but was replaced by the word 'Austria.' At the risk of encountering criticism by constitutional purists I shall follow this usage. This will not prevent me from continuing, for reasons of linguistic simplicity, to use the term 'Austria' (rather than the official designation 'Austro-Hungarian Monarchy' established in 1867) when speaking of the Empire as a whole. I trust the context will make it clear which of the two meanings is intended in any given case.
25 De Pretis's note to Beust of 1 May 1867: HHStA, Administrative Registratur, F34, Sonderreihe, Karton 41, 2. Teil.
26 Mallet's report to Lord Stanley of 18 June 1867: PRO, FO 425/90.
27 Mallet's report to Lord Stanley of 11 June 1867: ibid.

in a confidential conversation with Louis Mallet,[28] but a few days later were set forth officially by Beust in a note to Lord Bloomfield[29] and in an instruction for Count Apponyi in London.[30] Thus the British learnt that an important question connected with the Austro-Hungarian settlement was yet to be decided, namely whether treaties, or at all events commercial treaties affecting financial matters (such as the tariff), would in future have to be submitted before ratification for approval both to the Austrian *Reichsrat* and the Hungarian *Reichstag*. If the final version of the new constitution were to stipulate such a procedure – and Baron Beust expected that it would – the Imperial government would be ill advised at the present moment to conclude a treaty which they would have to submit to those two legislative bodies for assent. To do so in ignorance of their disposition and before the constitutional questions were settled – and this, Beust indicated, would take a few more months – would prejudice the Austro-Hungarian understanding.

These, briefly, were the Austrian arguments. They would have merited consideration had they been advanced in support of a request for British connivance at a delay in the execution of Article v of the December treaty, which called for the conclusion of a supplementary convention. Yet what Beust was offering was not arguments justifying the postponement of such a new treaty, but specious reasons for the non-fulfilment of an existing one. What he seemed to be urging – his note was not very specific on this point – was the indefinite adjournment or dissolution of the Mixed Commission, the body that was to have given substance to Articles iii and iv of the treaty of 1865. But this convention had, of course, long since been ratified *according to the constitution then in force,* and there could be no question of submitting it for approval to the legislatures of Austria and Hungary.

Baron Beust was too accomplished a diplomat not to have

28 Mallet's report to Lord Stanley of 3 July 1867: ibid.
29 Beust's note to Lord Bloomfield of 6 July 1867: ibid.
30 Instruction for Apponyi (draft) of 9 July 1867: HHStA, Administrative Registratur, F34, Sonderreihe, Karton 32, r2, Varia, 1. Teil.

recognized the flimsy nature of his arguments. In all likelihood they merely served the purpose of warning London that Austria had no intention of carrying out the provisions of the December treaty. Yet as the Minister responsible for his country's foreign relations, Beust was just as anxious as Rechberg and Mensdorff had been not to antagonize British public opinion: the onus of bringing about a rupture of the commercial negotiation had to be avoided at all costs. Perhaps, by offering them a face-saving alternative, the British government could be induced to forego their claim to a literal fulfilment of the treaty? It was with this possibility in mind that Baron Gagern, acting on Beust's orders, floated a *ballon d'essai*. In private conversations with Mallet he suggested that it might be possible 'to arrive at an understanding of a practical nature without awaiting the results of an agreement upon questions of detail which gave rise at every point to fresh and disagreeable controversy.'[31] More specifically, Gagern asked Mallet whether he could not prepare a confidential statement in which, without entering into the disputed questions of prices and averages, he could 'indicate the precise duties on the leading articles of British production which, in [his] opinion, Her Majesty's government might be induced to accept in fulfilment of the treaty.'[32] Mallet, even though, as he confided to Lord Stanley, he was convinced from the first day of his arrival at Vienna that it was 'only by some such compromise as this that any result [could] be obtained in a reasonable time,'[33] pretended to be reluctant to undertake the task Gagern wanted him to perform. In the end, however, he promised his Austrian colleague that he would endeavour to prepare such an outline of a practical arrangement which he might submit for consideration to his government, 'on the distinct understanding that any such private communication was not to be allowed to interfere in any way with the simultaneous prosecution of the work of the [Mixed] Commission.'[34] To Lord Stanley Mallet expressed the hope that his project 'might,

31 Mallet's report to Lord Stanley of 25 June 1867: PRO, FO 425/90.
32 Ibid.
33 Ibid.
34 Ibid.

perhaps, be made acceptable to both governments, and ..., while avoiding, on the one hand, the inconveniences which the Austrian government are obliged to consider, might nevertheless be such as to satisfy the just expectations of Parliament and the public in England.'[35]

Mallet set to work at once, and less than two weeks later, on 1 July, he communicated to Lord Stanley the fruit of his labours, the draft of an Austrian tariff which, although not drawn up with a view to literal fulfilment of the treaty stipulations, might nevertheless, he thought, be accepted by the British Cabinet as a reasonable equivalent. For the reduced duties which he sought to obtain were, except in the case of iron and cotton, in general accordance with the treaty: the maximum rate of 25 per cent would not be exceeded in the case of any important articles.[36] If approved, Mallet proposed to submit this project to the Austrian plenipotentiaries for negotiation.

The Board of Trade, invited by the Foreign Office to give their opinion on Mallet's project, endorsed his view that 'in order to show the willingness of Her Majesty's government to take all means in their power to meet the Austrian government and to arrive at a satisfactory settlement ... a specific proposal for new duties should be submitted to them in lieu of the method proposed by the treaty.'[37] In Vienna, however, Louis Mallet had meanwhile developed serious doubts about whether to communicate his project to the Austrians.[38] Having just been apprised by Baron Gagern of certain unresolved constitutional problems of the Habsburg monarchy (see above, p. 90f.) he could not but wonder whether under these circumstances it would serve any purpose to offer a settlement which, if it was to be made binding, would have to take the form of a treaty. Seeing that Beust for constitutional reasons considered himself unable to sign a convention, Mallet told Baron Gagern 'it would only be a waste of time to discuss the project.'[39] However a week later he changed his

35 Mallet's report to Lord Stanley of 25 June 1867: PRO, FO 425/90.
36 Mallet's report to Lord Stanley of 1 July 1867 with enclosure: ibid.
37 T.H. Farrer's note to Mr. Hammond of 9 July 1867: ibid.
38 Mallet's report to Lord Stanley of 3 July 1867: ibid.
39 Ibid.

mind and handed in his project after all.[40] Lord Stanley, on receipt of Mallet's report, wired his approval.[41]

In the meantime the Austrians on their part had taken the initiative in trying to find an escape from the impasse to which the negotiation had led. In a note addressed to Lord Bloomfield on 6 July 1867 Baron Beust offered to bind his government by a secret protocol 'to introduce the tariff modifications which, as a result of the Tariff Commission, they may recognize as necessary, as soon as the [constitutional] hindrances have been removed.'[42] This, of course, was not much of an offer. It certainly was far from being the 'equivalent' to Britain's specific and indisputable claims under the treaty of 1865 which Mallet had in mind. Austria's vague promise to liberalize her tariff would be only a contingent one, and its redemption might be postponed to the Greek Kalends. Moreover, as the Board of Trade pointed out in their comments on Beust's proposal, 'the treaty rights are binding on Austria as a nation, whilst such an undertaking would be binding on the Austrian Ministry only.'[43]

Not surprisingly, London rejected Beust's scheme out of hand. 'Her Majesty's government,' Lord Stanley informed Bloomfield, 'cannot consent to substitute the secret arrangement proposed to them by the Austrian government, to take effect at some future and indefinite time, for the arrangement which, according to the treaty, ought to take effect forthwith.'[44] But in view of Austria's constitutional difficulties, which Count Apponyi had recently explained to him in great detail,[45] the Foreign Secretary did not rule out a reasonable compromise based on Mallet's project of tariff modifications. He authorized Bloomfield to tell Baron Beust that 'in the event of [Austria's] showing a disposition to adopt the main points of Mr. Mallet's 'Project' in a fair and liberal

---

40 Mallet's report to Lord Stanley of 11 July 1867: ibid.
41 Lord Stanley's telegram to Bloomfield of 15 July 1867: ibid.
42 Beust's note to Bloomfield of 6 July 1867 (trans.), enclosed in the latter's dispatch of 9 July 1867: ibid.
43 T.H. Farrer's note to E.C. Egerton of 15 July 1867: ibid.
44 Instruction for Bloomfield of 23 July 1867: ibid.
45 See Apponyi's memorandum, enclosed in a second instruction for Bloomfield of 23 July 1867: ibid.

spirit, ... Her Majesty's government are prepared to waive the demand which, under the treaty, they might justly have insisted upon, of having those modifications recorded in a convention to take effect irrespective of any action on the part of the Austrian legislature.' London would have to insist, however, that those modifications be 'embodied in a supplementary convention, containing a formal pledge on the part of the Austrian government to submit it for approval of their legislature as soon as possible, and within a specified time.'[46]

Though Bloomfield had been ordered by Lord Stanley to communicate a copy of his dispatch to Baron Beust, he decided against this step. For in the meantime the acceptance by the Austrians of what he and Mallet regarded as the substance of the latter's project had suddenly created a new situation. As the Ambassador informed Stanley by ciphered telegram, the Austrian government were now ready to sign a protocol, not to be published for the present, by which they would pledge themselves *unconditionally* to introduce the tariff changes proposed by Mallet. These would come into force as soon as the constitutional difficulty was removed and the treaty with the *Zollverein* concluded, under no circumstances, however, later than 1 January 1869. As a further inducement Vienna offered to sign an Anglo-Austrian treaty of navigation without delay.[47] Bloomfield concluded his message with an urgent request for authority to sign the proposed protocol by Monday morning (29 July), seeing that Beust planned to leave Vienna the following day.[48]

The numerous dispatches sent to Lord Stanley in the course of the following weeks by Bloomfield and Mallet leave no doubt that the British negotiators regarded the compromise as a great success for their country. They extolled 'the character and extent of the new concessions which [they had] succeeded in securing'[49]

46 Instruction for Bloomfield of 23 July 1867: ibid.
47 The treaty, under which British vessels were admitted to the coasting trade and to the internal waters of the Empire, was signed at Vienna on 30 April, 1868 – not exactly 'without delay.' See *British and Foreign State Papers 1867–68*, LVIII, 11ff.
48 Bloomfield's telegraphic dispatch of 27 July 1867: PRO, FO 425/90.
49 Mallet's report of 29 July 1867: ibid.

– important reductions of duty on linens, metal wares, earthenware, india-rubber wares, oilcloth, paper, etc., as well as 'the application of optional *ad valorem* duties to cottons and woollens, a principle of customs taxation which has been hitherto resisted throughout Germany, and is one of the greatest value in international trade.'[50]

But the Foreign Office took a much less sanguine view of the matter. As might have been foreseen by Bloomfield, Lord Stanley categorically refused to give him and Mallet *carte blanche*. He informed the Ambassador by wire that he could not authorize him 'to sign a protocol ... without having the draft textually before [him], or without having before [him] the draft of navigation treaty the conclusion of which is to be promised in the proposed protocol.'[51] Nor was the Foreign Secretary's reluctance much diminished after he had seen the exact terms of the instruments in question. As he explained at length in a dispatch to Bloomfield, he could see no reason why the concessions to be recorded in a protocol should not come into operation at once; and he objected more particularly to the secrecy the Imperial government appeared to insist on. He rejected the argument that it was necessary to keep Austria's tariff reductions secret so as to enable her to strike a better bargain with the *Zollverein*. 'A secret engagement with Austria,' Stanley declared, 'such as is contemplated by the protocol, is ... wholly out of the question.'[52]

Bloomfield and Mallet on their part, anticipating, or replying to, Whitehall's criticism of their handiwork, were able to muster powerful arguments in favour of the protocol. They could not deny that its acceptance would mean agreeing to yet another postponement of, as well as to certain deviations from, the Austrian tariff reform stipulated by the treaty of 1865. But they stressed the important fact that under the protocol the Imperial government would assume an unconditional obligation to bring the reduced duties into force, irrespective of its ratification by

---

50 Ibid.
51 Stanley's telegram of 29 July 1867: ibid.
52 Instruction for Bloomfield of 9 August 1867: ibid.

the legislative bodies of the Empire.[53] Moreover, although the stipulations of Articles III and IV of the December treaty would not be literally executed, the sum of the advantages which would be extended to British trade under the protocol, Mallet insisted, 'must be considered as fully equivalent to the concessions which [the British government] had a treaty right to demand.'[54] Indeed the proposed arrangement was one which, as a whole, Mallet considered to be 'of a more liberal and favourable kind than would have resulted from an equitable, still less from a liberal execution of the IIIrd and IVth Articles of the treaty of 1865 by a ... Mixed Commission.'[55] 'Under its operation the Austrian tariff, instead of being one of the most obstructive and illiberal in Europe, [would] not only bear comparison with the reformed French and *Zollverein* tariffs, but [would] be in some not unimportant respects more favourable to trade than the former, and in its principal positions nearly identical with the latter, while in its application of the principle of optional *ad valorem* duties to the great categories of cotton and woollen tissues, it [would] have borrowed one of the most valuable features of the Belgian and Italian system.'[56] All in all, Bloomfield and Mallet were convinced that they had wrung a maximum of concessions from Austria, and that nothing would be gained from spinning out the negotiations. On the contrary, they thought it more than likely that delay would merely give the opponents of Free Trade in Austria a chance to reassert themselves. Though momentarily chastened by Beust's determination to bring about an Anglo-Austrian understanding, the protectionist bureaucracy, firmly entrenched in the Ministries of Commerce and Finance, would 'not unnaturally seek to recover the ground which they have lost by our appeal to M. de Beust; ... in the ensuing session of the *Reichsrat* a Minister of Commerce may be appointed who may entertain views far less liberal than that statesman, and ... thus the very valuable results obtained

53 Mallet's report to Lord Stanley of 29 July 1867: ibid.
54 Mallet's report to Lord Stanley of 6 August 1867: ibid.
55 Ibid.
56 Ibid.

by the long and anxious labours of the last three months may be altogether lost.'[57]

Yet the spate of dispatches produced by the British commissioners failed to persuade their government of the merits of the scheme. Though Lord Stanley at last admitted that substantial benefits were likely to accrue to British trade from the promised reduction of the Austrian duties, and though he even held out the prospect of the Cabinet's agreeing to the later date for bringing the new rates into operation, he was adamant in his refusal to accept the condition of secrecy. 'The Parliament and the commercial public of this country,' he wrote to Bloomfield, 'cannot and will not be left uninformed of the true position of so important a matter, and therefore whatever Her Majesty's government assent to must be made public.'[58]

Unable to sway the Foreign Office and the Board of Trade by means of written communications, Bloomfield and Mallet decided to dispatch Robert Morier to London, in the hope that their junior colleague, by pleading in person for acceptance of their proposal, might have better success.[59] They were not disappointed. On his arrival at London Morier produced another draft of the protocol, a revised version of the one which Bloomfield had submitted two weeks before[60] but which had been turned down by the government. The new text[61] differed from the earlier one in one respect only: it contained no explicit reference to

---

57 Mallet's second report to Lord Stanley of 6 August 1867: ibid.
58 Instruction for Bloomfield of 9 August 1867: ibid.
59 Bloomfield's dispatch of 11 August 1867: ibid. Morier obviously shared his colleagues' impatience with Whitehall. In a letter to his father, written a few days before his departure from Vienna, he unburdened himself as follows: 'I have gradually got used to ... getting the most splendid successes for the F.O. and after they have been perfectly apathetic for ten weeks, seeing them flare up and determined on fighting, when the fight is over, the victory won, and their only business is to sit down and enjoy the fruits. Such is bureaucracy – always running after the shadow and missing the substance' (Rosslyn Wemyss [i.e., Victoria Wemyss, Baroness Wester-Wemyss], *Memoirs and Letters of the Right Hon. Sir Robert Morier, G.C.B.* (London, 1911), II. 107).
60 Enclosed in Bloomfield's dispatch of 30 July 1867: PRO, FO 425/90.
61 Enclosed in Stanley's instruction for Bloomfield of 21 August 1867: ibid.

secrecy, the one condition which London had found wholly unacceptable. On the contrary, it stated that 'Her Majesty's government [must] be placed in a position to communicate the then state of the negotiations to Parliament on its reassembling.' This stipulation, though it implied that the protocol would not be published at once, appears to have satisfied the Cabinet: the Board of Trade withdrew its objection to the protocol,[62] and Lord Stanley authorized Bloomfield and Mallet to sign it.[63]

From the point of view of the Austrians the revised version of the protocol left little to be desired. They would obtain an extension by one year of the period within which, under the protocol of 2 July 1866, they would have had to introduce major tariff reductions; and while they had not been able to secure a formal promise of secrecy from the British government they were given to understand that the agreement would not be made publicly known before the reassembling of Parliament – in February 1868 – and perhaps not even then. Lord Stanley explicitly authorized Morier to reassure Vienna on this point. 'Both the government and the public of Great Britain,' he was to declare, 'regard it as a matter of good faith that the details of a negotiation should not be made public so long as the negotiation is not terminated.[64] (This enigmatic reference to unfinished diplomatic business becomes intelligible in the light of the protocol, which stipulated for the adjournment to 1 January 1868 of the current negotiation, although, once the protocol was signed, there obviously remained no questions to be settled. The Austrians could not fail to understand that this formal adjournment of a completed negotiation was a piece of legal fiction, devised by the British government to justify, if necessary, a belated publication of the agreement.)

A minor matter – it concerned the Austrian duty on chloride of lime – having been disposed of, the protocol was signed on

---

62 Robert G.W. Herbert's note to Mr Egerton of 19 August 1867: ibid.
63 Stanley's instruction for Bloomfield of 21 August 1867: ibid.
64 Morier's memorandum of 22 August 1867: ibid. See also his private letter to Baron Gagern of 27 August 1867: ibid.

8 September 1867.[65] Simultaneously with the signature Lord Bloomfield and Baron Beust exchanged notes[66] meant further to clarify the question of publicity. The Ambassador reaffirmed the intention of his government, 'in the improbable and unexpected event of the Austrian government not having wholly surmounted their difficulties,' to give Parliament by the time it reassembles 'a clear and explicit account of the actual state of the negotiation.' Beust on behalf of the Imperial government expressed his 'distinct consent' to this procedure. Though still reluctant to have Austria's tariff concessions made public, he could well afford to do so. For the wording of Bloomfield's note – it must have been concerted beforehand – indicated quite clearly that in case the British government were to render an account to Parliament they would stick to generalities and not reveal any details of the tariff changes agreed upon.

Beust's trust in Lord Stanley's discretion was not misplaced: anxious to avoid causing embarrassment to the Austrian government, the Foreign Secretary altogether refrained from reporting to Parliament on the state of the negotiation, even though 'the improbable and unexpected event' referred to in his note of 8 September had come to pass, and he would therefore have been free to disclose the contents of the protocol. When on 21 May 1868 Mr W.E. Forster raised a question in the House of Commons regarding the date when the Anglo-Austrian treaty of Commerce would come into operation Stanley answered evasively. 'He regretted to state,' he said, 'that the negotiations on this subject had not yet been brought to a final conclusion; ... but he hoped before long to be able to give the hon. gentleman and the House more ample and satisfactory information on the subject than he could do at present.'[67] Yet even after the Anglo-Austrian negotiations were concluded with the signature of a supplementary convention (see below, p. 111) the Foreign Secretary remained studi-

65 Bloomfield's dispatch of 8 September 1867 with enclosures: ibid. The Austrian duplicate of the instrument in HHStA, Administrative Registratur, F34, Sonderreihe, Karton 32, r2, 1 Varia, 1. Teil.
66 Enclosed in Bloomfield's dispatch of 8 September 1867: PRO, FO 425/90.
67 *Parliamentary Debates* (Hansard), 3rd s., vol. CXCII, cols. 652f.

ously secretive. In compliance with Beust's urgent request he even shelved the fulfilment of a promise given in his absence to the Commons by E.C. Egerton, his Undersecretary, who in reply to a question had rashly offered 'to lay on the table not only the valuable reports of Mr. Morier and Mr. Mallet, but also any other correspondence relating to the subject.'[68] When Baron Beust, greatly alarmed at this prospect, instructed Count Apponyi to protest against a premature disclosure of the terms of the convention, which was yet to be ratified,[69] Stanley hastened to reassure him that 'there [was] at present no intention on the part of Her Majesty's government of communicating to Parliament the correspondence connected with this negotiation.'[70]

68 Ibid., vol. cxciii, cols. 515f. (2 July 1868).
69 See Beust's telegraphic instruction for Apponyi of 4 July 1868 (draft): HHStA, Administrative Registratur, F34, Sonderreihe, Karton 32, r2, 1 Varia, 2. Teil. See also Bloomfield's dispatch of 6 July 1868: PRO, FO 425/91.
70 Bloomfield's dispatch of 14 July 1868: ibid. See also Apponyi's dispatch of 7 July 1868: HHStA, Administrative Registratur, F34, Sonderreihe, Karton 32, r2, 1 Varia, 2. Teil.

6

A supplementary convention

As far as the diffusion of Free Trade policies was concerned, the most-favoured-nation clause, which by the 1860s had come to be inserted as a matter of course into all commercial treaties, tended to work both ways. On the one hand it promoted the dismantling of Protection in that it at once extended to all nations with which a country had commercial agreements any tariff reductions which it conceded to another party. On the other hand, this very automatism, as has been shown above (p. 84), could have serious inhibitory effects. Since under the most-favoured-nation arrangement a country would have to grant to others *without any quid pro quo* benefits which it was willing to concede only as a matter of reciprocity, negotiators were reluctant to make concessions which would deprive them of bargaining counters in future deals with other States. This could and did result in frustration and delays. Thus, in 1867, when Franco-Prussian parleys became stalled over the duties on French wine, the negotiation of a Prusso-Austrian treaty of commerce, which had been resumed in the summer,[1] also fell into abeyance.[2] This in turn was the main though not the only reason why the Austrian government refused to come to a final arrangement with Britain.

1 Mallet's report to Lord Stanley of 8 September 1867: PRO, FO 425/90.
2 Lord Augustus Loftus's dispatch from Berlin of 26 October 1867: PRO, FO 425/91.

Of this chain of causation Bloomfield was fully aware. When by December 1867 it became obvious that Austria's treaty with Prussia would not be concluded before the end of the year, the Ambassador pointed out that for the time being a meeting of the British and Austrian plenipotentiaries, such as was stipulated for by the protocol of 8 September, would be premature: it would, he wrote to Lord Stanley, 'assuredly lead to a renewal of the difficulties we have hitherto had to contend with.' He therefore suggested that 'Her Majesty's government should not press the matter until the Austrian and Prussian convention is concluded.'[3] The Board of Trade and the Foreign Office accepted this advice all the more readily since there were indications that the diplomatic log jam was at long last breaking up. 'As there seems every reason to believe,' Lord Stanley wrote to Bonar, 'that the pending negotiations between France and Prussia, and Prussia and Austria, will be concluded in a few weeks, it will be better that the meeting [of the plenipotentiaries] should be postponed.'[4]

As a matter of fact after a last-minute hitch[5] the Franco-Prussian treaty of commerce was signed on 25 January 1868,[6] whereupon the Austrian government at once sent M. de Pretis to Berlin with orders to resume the commercial negotiations with Prussia.[7] Everybody expected that these talks would be of short duration, and Baron Beust let it be known that the negotiation with Britain would recommence immediately upon Pretis's return.[8] And so it fell out: the Austrian treaty with Prussia was signed on 9 March,[9] and Beust lost no time informing the British Chargé d'Affaires that the Imperial government were now ready 'at any time, counting from the 30th day of the current month of March, to resume negotiations with Her Britannic Majesty's plenipotentiaries for

3 Bloomfield's dispatch of 16 December 1867: ibid.
4 Instruction for Bonar of 24 December 1867: ibid. See also T.H. Farrer's letter to Mr Hammond of 23 December 1867: ibid.
5 Lord Augustus Loftus's dispatch from Berlin of 11 January 1868: ibid.
6 Bonar's dispatch of 28 January 1868: ibid.
7 Bonar's dispatch of 4 February 1868: ibid.
8 Ibid.
9 Bonar's dispatch of 9 March 1868: ibid.

the conclusion of a supplementary convention and of a navigation treaty.'[10] Things seemed to be moving very smoothly indeed. 'Considering,' Beust added, 'that the agreements already arrived at, on the 8th of September last, with regard to the tariff require only to be put into the form of a convention; and that the principal stipulations of the navigation treaty have already been discussed in anticipation between the plenipotentiaries of both parties, the whole negotiation might, if so required, be completed in fourteen days.'[11]

However the diplomatic sky, which had cleared momentarily, rapidly clouded over again. No sooner had Louis Mallet arrived at Vienna for the purpose of converting the protocol of 8 September into a convention than Baron Beust confronted him and Lord Bloomfield with a proposal which, though not wholly unexpected, nevertheless created consternation. What the Foreign Minister asked for was nothing less than the elimination from the text of the forthcoming treaty of the one Austrian concession recorded in the September protocol to which the British attached the greatest importance, namely the application of optional *ad valorem* duties to cotton and woollen tissues.[12]

It is safe to assume that Beust made this proposal with some reluctance. He cannot have doubted for a moment that his demand, however tentative, would create acute ill-feeling in London and might, if insisted upon, lead to a rupture of the negotiation. But he was bowing to heavy political pressure. The Hungarian government, to be sure, were all in favour of liberalizing the economic policy of the Empire; they welcomed the proposed treaty with Britain, and promised to submit it to their legislature with a strong recommendation for adoption.[13] The Austrian Cabinet, however, disapproved of the concessions made to Britain

10 Beust's note to Bonar of 9 March 1868: ibid.
11 Ibid.
12 Mallet's report to Lord Stanley of 31 March 1868: ibid.
13 The decision of the Hungarian Cabinet was communicated to Beust by the Premier Count Julius Andrássy in his note of 26 April 1868: HHStA, Administrative Registratur, F34, Sonderreihe, Karton 32, r2, 1 Varia, 1. Teil.

under the September protocol, and did not wish to see them reaffirmed in the more solemn form of a convention. The most determined opponent of such a treaty was Ignaz von Plener, who had been given the portfolio of Commerce when Prince Carlos Auersperg's 'Ministry of Bourgeois' took office at the beginning of 1868. He knew only too well how difficult it would be for him to defend the pending convention before the *Reichsrat*, a legislative body whose majority was wedded to a policy of Protection.[14] Even the recently concluded commercial treaty with Prussia and the *Zollverein* was expected to, and in the event did, run into criticism in the Austrian Chamber, though in this case protectionist prejudice was outweighed by the desire to strengthen the Empire's ties with Germany.[15]

The British government were fully aware of Beust's domestic difficulties, but they refused to renounce claims the validity of which could not possibly be impugned. In his instruction for Bloomfield of 3 April 1868 Lord Stanley roundly declared that the proposed excision of the clause referring to the *ad valorem* duties 'could not be accepted by Her Majesty's government.'[16] The Foreign Secretary was all the less prepared to yield since Louis Mallet assured him that the Austrian legislature, if put to the test, would hardly take upon itself the responsibility of repudiating, by implication, a ratified international agreement, i.e., the treaty of 1865. After all, the supplementary convention for the conclusion of which he and Bloomfield had been invited to Vienna was nothing more than the execution of Articles III and IV of that treaty as amended by the protocol of 8 September 1867.[17] Intelligence imparted to Mallet by members of the *Reichsrat* seemed to confirm his assessment of the political situation. They had assured him that 'the suggested hostility to *ad*

14 Bloomfield's dispatch of 7 April 1868: PRO, FO 425/91.
15 See Adolf Beer, *Die österreichische Handelspolitik im neunzehnten Jahrhundert* (Vienna, 1891), pp. 382f.
16 PRO, FO 425/91.
17 Mallet's report to Lord Stanley of 7 April 1868: ibid. See also Count Apponyi's dispatch of 14 April 1868: HHStA, Administrative Registratur, F34, Sonderreihe, Karton 32, r2, 1 Varia, 1. Teil.

valorem duties existed far more in the [Austrian] Ministries of Commerce and Finance than in the legislature.'[18]

There is evidence to show that Baron Beust at this juncture did his level best to overcome what Morier described as 'the never-ceasing, never-resting hostility of the Ministry of Commerce to the engagement.'[19] Having failed in his halfhearted effort to obtain London's consent to the omission of the *ad valorem* options, a concession which, if granted, would in all likelihood have made the supplementary convention acceptable to Plener and his senior officials, the Foreign Minister tried another tack: he decided to enlist the monarch in support of his policy. At his suggestion the Emperor summoned Plener to Buda, where the Court was in residence at the time.[20] Obviously an attempt was to be made to prevail upon the refractory Minister to give up his opposition. So confident was Beust of success that he assured Lord Bloomfield that 'the difficulties in the way of completing the convention might be considered as removed ... He [Beust] trusted he should [on his return from Buda] find the members of the [Austrian] Council [of Ministers] fully prepared to agree to the convention, and, their sanction once obtained, ... there would be no further delay in signing it.'[21]

We do not know what happened during Plener's sojourn at Buda. One thing, however, is certain: after the conspicuous failure of Francis Joseph's neo-absolutist regime his resolve to abide by the rules of constitutional government had become unshakeable.[22] Beust, who ought to have known better, was mistaken in

18 Mallet's letter to Bloomfield of 17 April 1868: PRO, FO 425/91.
19 Minutes of a conversation between Mallet and Count Vitzthum, drawn up by Morier and enclosed in Mallet's report to Lord Stanley of 29 April 1868: ibid.
20 Beust's letter to Francis Joseph of 12 April 1868 (draft in Beust's handwriting): HHStA, Administrative Registratur, F34, Sonderreihe, Karton 32, r2, 1 Varia, 1. Teil.
21 Bloomfield's dispatch of 14 April 1868: PRO, FO 425/91. See also Mallet's private letter to Mr Egerton of the same date and his report to Lord Stanley of 21 April 1868: ibid.
22 A book published by one of Beust's intimates under the *nom de plume* of

his expectation that the Emperor would do more than use some mild persuasion, or that Plener would let himself be overawed by the sovereign. As a matter of fact the Minister's opposition to the supplementary convention continued unabated and was fully endorsed by his colleagues: on 24 April Beust informed Lord Bloomfield that the Austrian Council of Ministers had finally decided to reject the treaty unless the *ad valorem* duties on cottons were omitted.[23]

The British plenipotentiaries, who had been led to believe that the sanction of the convention by the Austrian Ministry was assured, were taken aback by this turn of events. Louis Mallet in particular was greatly upset and angered, and requested permission to return to London unless a satisfactory settlement were obtained within forty-eight hours.[24] 'A further acquiescence in the course pursued by the Austrian government,' he wrote to Lord Stanley, 'appears to me inconsistent with a due regard to the dignity of Her Majesty's government and to my own character.'[25] Beust was hardly less disconcerted. Under no circumstances, he confided to Baron Gagern, would he identify himself with the decision of the Austrian Council of Ministers; he would confine himself to informing the British government of what had

---

'An Englishman' (*The Austro-Hungarian Empire and the Policy of Count Beust*, London, 1870) stressed that 'the Emperor, from the moment when he wisely decided that absolutism should make way for Parliamentary rule, unflinchingly and consistently maintained and facilitated the latter system of government' (p. 36). In his introduction to the English edition of Beust's *Memoirs* the Anglo-German banker Baron Henry de Worms, MP, revealed his authorship of that fulsome panegyric upon Beust, but failed to acknowledge that it was for the most part the handiwork of the Chancellor's own press bureau; see Ernst Freiherr von Plener, *Erinnerungen* (Stuttgart & Leipzig, 1911), I, 344.

23 Bloomfield's telegraphic dispatch of 25 April 1868: PRO, FO 425/91. For pure woollens and certain kinds of mixed tissues the *ad valorem* option stipulated in the September protocol was conceded. See Count Taaffe's note to Beust of 24 April 1868: HHStA, Administrative Registratur, F34, Sonderreihe, Karton 32, r2, 1 Varia, 1. Teil.

24 Bloomfield's telegraphic dispatch of 25 April 1868: PRO, FO 425/91.

25 Mallet's report to Lord Stanley of 28 April 1868: ibid.

happened.[26] For a moment even Plener seems to have been worried about the prospect of a rupture of the negotiation, which, he knew, would seriously strain Anglo-Austrian relations. 'Why did the *Reichskanzler* [i.e., Beust],' he complained to Gagern, 'ask us [the Austrian Ministry] instead of signing? We could have taken a chance and presented [the convention] to the *Reichsrat* as a *fait accompli*.'[27] (Beust must have considered this tactics, but rejected it. 'What good would it have done to England,' he wrote to Count Apponyi retrospectively, 'had I prevailed upon the [Austrian] Ministry to submit the convention to the *Reichstag* at a venture, or rather in the certainty of having it rejected?'[28])

Despite the miscarriage of his policy Beust did not offer his resignation. He did not despair of mending matters if only the threatened rupture of the negotiation could be averted. But having had to depart for Buda on important business of State, he could not himself undertake this urgent task. He entrusted the delicate job of pacifying the outraged Mallet and his colleagues to Count Vitzthum, a diplomat chosen 'because of his experience in dealing with the English and his friendship with Morier.'[29]

By the time the Count began his talks with the British representatives, the danger of an imminent diplomatic breakdown had already receded: Lord Stanley in a telegraphic message to Bloomfield had expressed his wish that Mallet should for the

26 Beust's telegram to Gagern of 25 April 1868: HHStA, Administrative Registratur, F34, Sonderreihe, Karton 32, r2, 1 Varia, 1. Teil. To dissociate himself from the decision of the Austrian Council of Ministers did not make Beust guilty of a breach of Cabinet solidarity. After the consitutional reform of December 1867 he and his successors at the head of the Imperial Ministry of Foreign Affairs were members neither of the Austrian nor of the Hungarian Ministry.
27 Meysenbug's telegram to Beust of 27 April 1868 (draft; trans.): ibid.
28 Instruction for Apponyi of 5 May 1868 (draft; trans.): ibid.
29 Beust's telegram to Meysenbug of 27 April 1868 (draft in Beust's handwriting; trans.): ibid. See also Beust's letter to Bloomfield of the same date: ibid. Count Karl Friedrich Vitzthum von Eckstädt, the Austrian Minister Plenipotentiary to Belgium, was indeed well qualified for his task. He had held the post of Saxon Minister to the Court of St James from 1853 to 1867. He then, following the example of his chief, Baron Beust, entered the Austrian service; see *Allgemeine deutsche Biographie*, LV, 341ff.

time being remain in Vienna.[30] The forbearance of the Foreign Secretary appeared to be fully justified when Count Vitzthum at his very first meeting with the British representatives disclosed that Beust, notwithstanding the negative attitude of the Austrian Ministry, had decided to sign the supplementary convention in complete conformity with the protocol of 8 September 1867, that is to say without omission of the *ad valorem* options. Only he could not do so at once: in view of grave parliamentary difficulties the signature would have to be postponed by a few weeks, until after the adjournment of the *Reichsrat*.[31]

Beust's domestic troubles, which served as an excuse for such a delay, were real enough. He was known to have made strenuous efforts to win papal acquiescence in the rescinding of Austria's concordat with the Holy See. More recently he had been instrumental in securing the passage through the Upper House of laws that flagrantly contravened some important provisions of that concordat, and he was suspected of using his influence with the reluctant Emperor to obtain his assent to those pieces of legislation.[32] All this had made Beust – a Lutheran – an object of hatred to the ultramontane Court party, while the more extreme liberals accused him of timidity and weakness in these matters.[33] In these circumstances, Count Vitzthum assured Lord Bloomfield, signing the unpopular treaty with Britain would make Beust's political position untenable: he simply could not afford to antagonize the *Reichsrat*. The 'Court party [is] watching the first opportunity of a quarrel between him and the *Reichsrat*, to step in and seize on the reins, and overthrow all he has been building up. Baron

---

30 Stanley's telegram to Bloomfield of 27 April 1868: PRO, FO 425/91.
31 Bloomfield's dispatch of 29 April 1868: ibid. See also his telegraphic dispatch of 1 May 1868: ibid.
32 Beust boasted in his autobiography that 'it was entirely and exclusively [his] doing that the religious laws were sanctioned [by the Emperor] and passed through the Upper House' (Friedrich Ferdinand Count von Beust, *Memoirs*, 2nd ed. [London, 1887], II, 71f.). See also Erika Weinzierl-Fischer, *Die österreichischen Konkordate von 1855 und 1933* (Vienna, 1960), pp. 108f.
33 Beust, II, 74.

Beust therefore makes an appeal *ad misericordiam* to the British government for a delay of some weeks in signing the commercial convention, for the purpose of enabling him to get through his Parliamentary difficulties.'[34]

Count Vitzthum's assurance that Beust was still determined to sign the supplementary convention, albeit at a later date, and his announcement that the treaty of navigation was ready for immediate signature[35] did something to assuage the temper of Mallet and his colleagues.[36] Still, after all that had happened since 1865, they could hardly avoid being suspicious of yet another delay. It would, Mallet told Beust on his return from Buda, 'excite the greatest disappointment in England, and cause a well-founded distrust on the part of Her Majesty's government as to the real intention on the part of His Excellency to stand by the engagements of the protocol.'[37] In this context Mallet asked two blunt questions of the Minister: 'What was the period to which he proposed to defer the signature?' And, 'What were the grounds upon which he based a reasonable expectation in that he should be better able to fulfil his engagements at that period than at present?'[38] Beust replied that he would propose a delay of six weeks.

As regards the prospect ... of his being in a better position for concluding the negotiation at a future time than at present, he could only say that he had reason to think that, when the grave questions now before the *Reichsrat* and the country were satisfactorily settled, and time had been

---

34 Bloomfield's dispatch of 29 April 1868: PRO, FO 425/91. See also Mallet's report to Lord Stanley of 1 May 1868: ibid.

35 It was signed on Beust's return to Vienna, in the evening of 30 April 1868. See Beust's note of invitation to Bloomfield of that date (draft): HHStA, Administrative Registratur, F34, Sonderreihe, Karton 32, r2, 1 Varia, 1. Teil. The ratifications were exchanged on 26 June 1868; see Beust's note to Bloomfield of 25 June 1868 (draft): ibid., 2. Teil.

36 On 28 April 1868, after his first meeting with the British, Vitzthum, much encouraged, sent a wire to Beust, assuring him that 'Bloomfield, Mallet and Morier [had] calmed down' (draft in Vitzthum's handwriting): ibid., 1. Teil.

37 Mallet's report to Lord Stanley of 1 May 1868: PRO, FO 425/91.

38 Ibid.

given to allow of the inquiries which the Council of Ministers insisted
on making as to the effect of the proposed *ad valorem* duties, he should
be able to find the means of obtaining a sufficient measure of support
from members of the government to carry the question successfully in
the Chamber and to redeem his pledge.[39]

Mallet and Bloomfield were favourably impressed by the tone
and language of Baron Beust, more especially by his emphatic
and repeated assurance that he was 'prepared after the present
session [of the *Reichsrat*], if necessary, to provoke a rupture with
his recalcitrant Ministers,'[40] that 'he had assured himself of the
Emperor's support, and ... that he would make [the ratification
of the treaty] a Cabinet question.'[41]

At the Foreign Office, meanwhile, Vienna's latest moves had
created bitter resentment. 'If Lord Stanley had followed the advice
of Mr. Hammond [the Undersecretary of State],' Count Apponyi
reported to Beust, 'the negotiation would by now have been
broken off with *éclat*.'[42] Stanley himself made no attempt to hide
his irritation from the Ambassador, and threatened to disclose
the whole story of Austria's discreditable behaviour to Parliament.
In the end, however, more moderate councils prevailed. Having
listened to the oral reports of Mallet, who had returned to London
on 8 May,[43] Lord Stanley decided to agree to the requested postponement of the signature and instructed Bloomfield accordingly.[44] It was on 1 July, only a little later than Beust had promised
originally, that the supplementary convention was signed and
sealed.[45]

39 Ibid.
40 Ibid.
41 Bloomfield's dispatch of 1 May 1868: ibid.
42 Apponyi's dispatch of 6 May 1868: HHStA, Administrative Registratur, F34,
   Sonderreihe, Karton 32, r2, 1 Varia, 1. Teil (trans.). See also his private letter
   to Beust of the same date: ibid., 2. Teil.
43 Stanley's telegram to Bloomfield of 8 May 1868: PRO, FO 425/91.
44 Instruction for Bloomfield of 12 May 1868: ibid.
45 The original of the Austrian copy of the treaty is to be found in HHStA, Administrative Registratur, F34, Sonderreihe, Karton 32, r2, 1 Varia, 2. Teil.

7

A new treaty

When Baron Beust, anxious to avoid a rupture of the negotiation, offered to sign the supplementary convention, he did so on his own responsibility, without having obtained the approval of the Austrian Ministry. But before he put his signature to the document he deemed it advisable to inform his colleagues of his decision, and to expound his reasons for taking it. In an official note addressed to the Austrian Minister of Commerce[1] Beust declared that he regarded himself 'both entitled and obliged to sign.' The British claims, he argued, were unassailable. They were based on the treaty of commerce of 16 December 1865 and on the protocol of 8 September 1867, international agreements the validity of which was indisputable. The latter, a compromise for which he, Beust, after consultation with the Ministers of Commerce and Finance had himself assumed responsibility, could not be made the object of further chaffering: it was the best bargain that was to be had. Since Austria's recent treaty with the German Customs Union had just become operative, Britain, by virtue of the most-favoured-nation clause of the December treaty, was already enjoying the reduced rates of duty stipulated in the pending convention. As for the controversial *ad valorem* options, Beust was able to remind Plener of expert evidence in his hands which

1 Beust's note to Ignaz von Plener of 28 June 1868 (draft): HHStA, Administrative Registratur, F34, Sonderreihe, Karton 32, r2, 1 Varia, 2. Teil.

must have set him at ease about the threat they were believed
to pose to the Austrian woollen and cotton industries. These
matters, Beust suggested, should be properly explained to the
public before the autumn session of the *Reichsrat*. If this were
done, if the Austrian government were to use the press to create
a climate of opinion favourable to the supplementary convention,
its rejection by the legislature need no longer be feared.

Plener replied to this note[2] with glacial reserve. So far from
endorsing Beust's decision to sign, he even refrained from criticiz-
ing it. His demonstrative *insouciance* could hardly be misunder-
stood. It was meant to remind the Minister of Foreign Affairs
that his signature was immaterial: the fate of the supplementary
convention would have to be decided by a vote of the *Reichsrat*.
So as to remove the slightest doubt on this score Plener found
it necessary to challenge Beust's opinion that under the provisions
of the Austro-Hungarian settlement of 1867 the September protocol, like all other international agreements concluded by Imperial governments prior to the constitutional reform, was binding
on both halves of the Empire. That protocol, Plener argued, could
not be classified as a State treaty; moreover, its very existence
had been unknown at the time when the new constitutional arrangements were arrived at.

Plener need not have worried about any sinister intentions
of the Foreign Minister. It is conceivable that at one time or
another Beust may indeed have toyed with a plan of bypassing
the two legislatures of the Empire and of proceeding immediately
to the ratification of the supplementary convention by the
monarch. After all this treaty would not create any new obligations: it merely repeated the stipulations of the September protocol, whose binding power the Minister had always asserted.
But if such an idea had ever crossed his mind Beust had by
now abandoned it. As a matter of fact, with a view to making
it possible for the convention to be debated and voted on during
the autumn session of the *Reichsrat*, he asked for and readily
obtained British consent to a generous extension of the eight

2 Plener's note to Beust of 1 July 1868: ibid.

weeks' term stipulated for the exchange of the ratification in Article x of the treaty.[3]

On October 17, in the first sitting of the Austrian Chamber after its summer recess, Ignaz von Plener laid upon the table of the House the supplementary convention, accompanied by a report of his own recommending its ratification. On this occasion A.G.G. Bonar, the British Chargé d'Affaires, inquired of Baron Beust 'whether, with the present attitude of parties in the Chamber, he could foresee with certainty the result of the debate.'[4] The answer, though guarded, was reassuring. He expected, Beust said, the *ad valorem* clause to give rise to an animated discussion and some opposition, but he was convinced that it would ultimately be carried. The other provisions of the treaty were not likely to be attacked. A few days later, in reply to a private letter of Bonar,[5] the Foreign Minister was a little more specific. '*J'ai lieu d'espérer,*' he wrote, '*que la convention sera votée à Vienne comme à Pesth, si non avant le 1er novembre du moins dans la première quinzaine du mois, et je m'empresserai de la soumettre à la ratification de Sa Majesté l'Empereur et Roi dès que les votes seront assurés.*'[6]

Soon afterwards, however, the news from Vienna became rather disquieting. On 3 November Bonar reported[7] that the convention was running into strong opposition in the Finance Committee of the *Reichsrat*, to which it had been referred. Beust still pretended to be hopeful of its ultimate adoption by the Chamber, but petitions demanding its rejection were coming in from various quarters, among them appeals from the Minister's own constituents. Three days later Beust admitted to the Chargé d'Affaires that 'if [the] convention were now forced before the House there could not be a doubt of its unconditional rejection.'[8] The Austrian Ministry, he explained, was in the throes of a serious parliamen-

---

3 See Beust's note to Bloomfield of 1 July 1868 (draft): ibid., and Stanley's instruction for Bloomfield of the same date: PRO, FO 425/91.
4 Bonar's dispatch to Stanley of 20 October 1868: ibid.
5 Bonar's letter to Beust of 23 October 1868: HHStA, Administrative Registratur, F34, Sonderreihe, Karton 32, r2, 1 Varia, 2. Teil.
6 Beust's note to Bonar of 26 October 1868: PRO, FO 425/91.
7 Bonar's dispatch of 3 November 1868: ibid.
8 Bonar's dispatch of 6 November 1868: ibid.

tary crisis over a bill providing for a common army for the whole Empire. Its passage by a narrow majority could be expected since the Cabinet had staked its existence on its adoption. But having defied the Chamber on this vital issue the government could not at this moment risk another battle over an equally unpopular measure. 'Seeing themselves compelled to pass the Military Bill, they [the Deputies] would wreak their vengeance on the convention ... It would be infallibly and unconditionally thrown out.'[9] Count Apponyi received instructions to offer similar explanations in London: he was to tell Lord Stanley that under the circumstances it would be imprudent to bring the supplementary convention to a vote in the *Reichsrat* before the middle of December.[10]

Though Beust assured the British that after a breathing space of only a few weeks the treaty would stand a better chance of being sanctioned he cannot have believed that. As a matter of fact he was already taking secret steps designed to make it virtually impossible for him to meet the December deadline. Acting in collusion with Count Andrássy, the Hungarian Premier, Beust made sure that the convention, though in no danger of being rejected, would not be presented to the Diet of Hungary in time to be dealt with by the legislature before its impending dissolution.[11] In a conversation with Stanley early in November Count Apponyi had already hinted at some such contingency. *'Je l'ai même preparé,'* he reported to Beust, *'à ce que, dans le cas le plus favorable, la convention ne pourrait devenir exécutoire que dans les pays en deça de la Leitha [i.e., in Austria], la diète hongroise devant être close le 10 décembre et les nouvelles Chambres ... ne pouvant se réunir avant le mois d'avril.'*[12] A week later Beust himself floated a similar *ballon d'essai*. In an interview with the British Chargé d'Affaires he gave to understand that 'after a certain interval ... he would have got rid of that host of angry opponents of the treaty who were now in person encamped at Vienna in order to use pressure upon their several

9 Ibid.
10 Instruction for Apponyi of 7 November 1868: HHStA, Administrative Registratur, F34, Sonderreihe, Karton 32, r2, 1 Varia, 2. Teil.
11 Andrássy's ciphered telegram to Beust of 14 November 1868: ibid.
12 Apponyi's dispatch of 10 November 1868: ibid.

Deputies. Three months hence it would be a comparatively easy matter to carry the bill; at present there was still great danger.'[13]

Reporting on this conversation Bonar felt obliged to emphasize that he had at no time 'been inclined to call in question in the slightest degree the sincerity and perfect good faith of Baron Beust.'[14] Our documentary evidence, however, does not bear out this generous testimonial. Just then the wily Minister was engaged in an elaborate game of deception. Though he had already made sure that the convention would not come to a vote in the Hungarian Diet before dissolution, he continued to assure Lord Stanley that the Austrian government were still resolved to place the convention before the *Reichsrat* by the middle of December, and that they would make every effort to promote its passage.[15] His real intentions, however, Beust revealed in a private letter to Apponyi.[16] He informed the Ambassador that all hopes of seeing the treaty accepted by the two legislative bodies had vanished, that he intended to obtain from the British government yet another deferment of six months, and that he planned to use this interval to gain London's consent to a radical revision of the provisions of the convention.

In his reply Count Apponyi expressed grave doubts about the chances of making the British government yield on these points. But Beust seems to have made up his mind, and in the course of the following year pursued his goal with a tenacity all the more remarkable since he was not ideologically committed to Protectionism by any means. On the contrary, in conversations with the British and – more convincingly – in his *Memoirs* he declared himself in sympathy with Free Trade, and strongly endorsed the orthodox arguments against Protection, 'a system which professes to protect native industry and at the same time raises the prices of all the necessaries of life for the working

13 Bonar's dispatch of 16 November 1868: PRO, FO 425/91.
14 Ibid.
15 Instruction for Apponyi of 24 November 1868 (draft): HHStA, Administrative Registratur, F34, Sonderreihe, Karton 32, r2, 1 Varia, 2. Teil.
16 This letter, dated 24 November 1868, is not extant. Its contents, however, can be inferred from Apponyi's reply of 1 December 1868: ibid.

man; a system which establishes new limitations for the protection of home produce, and yet removes from native industry the salutary influence of competition.'[17] In wresting commercial concessions from the British, Beust protests in his autobiography, he had to do violence to his own opinions. Yet he was vain enough to boast at the same time of having 'succeeded in performing a feat which has perhaps no precedent in the history of diplomacy: I prevailed upon the English government to alter the treaty which had already been signed, and to sign another.'[18]

The paths of diplomacy that Beust decided to follow in pursuit of this aim were long and tortuous. It was obvious that it would take time to wear down the resistance which the British government were sure to put up to a change of the convention. But Beust's ingenious scheme to gain half a year's respite by preventing it from being voted on by the Hungarian Diet threatened momentarily to miscarry when Bonar, alarmed by the prospect of yet a further delay, decided on 30 November 1868 'to go [himself] to Pesth immediately ... and to seek, through personal interviews with Count Andrássy and the Hungarian Minister of Commerce, to insure the convention being brought forward during the course of this week.'[19] The British Chargé d'Affaires no doubt greatly overrated his powers of persuasion; but Baron Beust was sufficiently worried by his intervention to make a strenuous effort to dissuade him from pressing the matter. He assured him – and the Hungarian Ministers confirmed his assessment of the political situation – that a previous vote by the Hungarian Diet in favour of the treaty would only strengthen the growing opposition in the *Reichsrat*, and – given Austrian jealousies – make its rejection a certainty. If, on the other hand, the Hungarian vote, whose favourable outcome was in no doubt, were to be postponed until the meeting of the new legislature in April, he, Beust, would bring the convention before the *Reichsrat* within a week, and 'he could positively engage that, with the indirect compensation

17 Friedrich Ferdinand Count von Beust, *Memoirs*, 2nd ed. (London, 1887), II, 95.
18 Ibid., II, 94.
19 Bonar's dispatch of 30 November 1868: PRO, FO 425/91.

conceded to Austria by the delay of the Hungarian vote, the convention would then be ratified by the *Reichsrat* and be passed at once, *pure et simple*, in all its present terms, unaltered and unconditionally.[20]

On the face of it Beust's proposition was certainly attractive. To be sure, the ratifications of the supplementary convention would not be exchanged, nor would its provisions become operative before April, when the Hungarian Diet was due to reassemble. Yet, if Beust could be trusted to make good his promise, the only serious stumbling block – an adverse vote of the Austrian legislature – would be cleared away within a matter of days, and the whole question would be completely set at rest. But was there any guarantee that the Minister would have his way with the Chamber? In the light of past experience doubts on this score were amply justified. 'I could not help reminding His Excellency,' Bonar reported to Lord Stanley, 'that on several previous occasions he had, though with the same sincere intentions, held the same language as now, and had believed himself in a position to justify the same formal pledge.'[21] Would he not again encounter insuperable obstacles? But Beust emphatically denied that there was any danger of being thwarted. 'With this additional and last concession,' he assured Bonar, 'I know my ground, and I give you my word of honour.'[22]

For a diplomat to receive a foreign statesman's personal word of honour was a singular experience; and Bonar, greatly impressed, could no longer doubt that Baron Beust would redeem a promise given in such solemn terms. He therefore decided to desist from further lobbying in the Hungarian capital, and returned to Vienna. 'The convention,' he cheerfully wired Lord Stanley, 'will come next week before the *Reichsrat*, and will be passed unaltered and unconditionally, and thus be finally settled as regards that portion of the Empire.'[23]

Yet the march of events almost at once belied Bonar's

20 Bonar's dispatch of 5 December 1868: ibid.
21 Bonar's dispatch of 6 December 1868: ibid.
22 Ibid.
23 Bonar's telegraphic dispatch of 6 December 1868: ibid.

optimism. On 18 December the Finance Committee of the *Reichsrat* after a lengthy debate unanimously adopted a motion asking the plenum to reject the supplementary convention in its present form, and to empower the government to open fresh negotiations with Britain, with a view to eliminating the *ad valorem* options and substituting for them a slight reduction of the specific duties on cotton and woollen tissues.[24]

Beust must have known for some time that the convention which he had signed the previous July had no chance of being accepted by the *Reichsrat*. As a matter of fact in a *dépêche ostensible* sent to Count Apponyi on 14 December[25] he did not repeat the pledge he had given to Bonar a week before, but merely promised that the Austrian government would make '*une effort suprême pour obtenir que la convention soit votée avant la fin de l'année courante.*' But, Beust added, the British government must surely realize '*qu'une transaction commerciale de la nature de notre convention supplémentaire, menaçant de nouvelles pertes et des plus graves dangers plusieurs de nos industries indigènes et introduisant une innovation dans notre système des droits d'entrée, doit ... courir aisément la mauvaise chance d'une discussion parlementaire.*'

This *dépêche ostensible* was accompanied by a confidential instruction for Apponyi[26] which reveals even more clearly that Beust, if he had ever counted on the *Reichsrat* to approve the supplementary convention, no longer entertained any such notion. The Austrian government, he told the Ambassador, had to contend with a growing mood of irritation among industrialists and politicians which made the rejection of the treaty a near certainty. The only chance of averting such an outcome might be an offer on the part of the British government to agree to a postponement

24 Bonar's dispatches of 16 and 18 December 1868 with enclosures: ibid.
25 Instruction for Apponyi of 14 December 1868: ibid.
26 Confidential instruction for Apponyi of 14 December 1868 (draft, partly in Beust's handwriting): HHStA, Administrative Registratur, F34, Sonderreihe, Karton 32, r2, 1 Varia, 2. Teil.

by one year of the coming into force of the contentious *ad valorem* clause, so that Austrian manufacturers could in the meantime accommodate themselves to the new conditions.

When Count Apponyi, on 22 December, called on Lord Clarendon, who a few days before had become Stanley's successor at the Foreign Office, his reception was a decidedly chilly one.[27] The Foreign Secretary at once cuttingly referred to Beust's failure to abide by his solemn engagement. Surely, he said, the difficulties which now served as an excuse for not fulfilling the promise of a favourable vote in the *Reichsrat* should have been foreseen: Beust ought never to have pledged his word of honour in a matter whose successful issue he could not count on with certainty. When he considered this whole business he, Clarendon, could not help doubting the sincerity of Austrian assurances.

Apponyi's position was not an enviable one. He could not possibly let Clarendon's strictures on the character of his chief pass unchallenged; yet he must have been at a loss to find convincing arguments in defense of Beust's behaviour. Nor could the Ambassador have felt comfortable when, in pursuance of Beust's recent suggestion, he next raised the question of a possible deferment of the *ad valorem* options. As a matter of fact the Foreign Secretary reacted quickly and vigorously to this proposal: its acceptance, he declared, after all that had happened, would make the British Cabinet a butt for general ridicule.

Yet their feeling of acute frustration did not prevent the British government from once more casting about for a compromise. Immediately after Apponyi's interview with Clarendon Lord Bloomfield received orders to propose to Count Beust[28] a solution which, since it would be only a literal fulfilment of a treaty already sanctioned, would not require consulting the *Reichsrat* and the Hungarian Diet. The Ambassador was to suggest that the Austrian government could redeem their pledges by reducing their specific duties on cottons and woollens to the level of those charged by

27 Apponyi's 'most confidential' dispatch of 22 December 1868: ibid.
28 An autograph letter addressed to Beust by the Emperor on 5 December 1868 informed him of his elevation to the rank of hereditary Count; see An Englishman [Henry de Worms], *The Austro-Hungarian Empire* (London, 1870), p. 305.

the German Customs Union. This the British government would accept in substitution for the *ad valorem* duties.[29]

Britain's conciliatory offer almost coincided with the above-mentioned resolution of the Finance Committee of the *Reichsrat* which authorized the Imperial government to open new negotiations with London 'on the basis that the tariff positions at present granted to the most favoured nation for cottons and woollens be lowered, on and after the 1st of January, 1870, to a rate which shall not exceed 20 per cent for cottons and 10 per cent for woollens, and under the condition that Articles III, IV and V of the treaty with Great Britain of the 16th of December, 1865, as well as Articles II and III of the Final Protocol [see above, pp. 79ff.] should be entirely set aside.'[30]

What Britain suggested as a quid pro quo if she were to relinquish her claim to the *ad valorem* options agreed upon under the protocol of 8 September 1867 and reconfirmed by Article III of the Supplementary Convention of 1 July 1868 – i.e., the immediate adoption by Austria of the *Zollverein* tariff for cottons and woollens – would, however, have required a much more substantial reduction of duties than that envisaged by the Finance Committee of the Austrian Chamber.[31] Thus when Lord Bloomfield presented Count Beust with the compromise proposal of his government, he was at once given to understand that it had no chance of being accepted. 'The great mass of the manufacturing interest,' the Chancellor declared, 'would ... be opposed to its adoption and would not be likely ... to agree to so large a reduction of duties.'[32] The British government on their part made it clear that they could not regard the proposals of the Finance Committee as satisfactory equivalents for the *ad valorem* options which they were asked to renounce, all the less so since

29 Instruction for Bloomfield of 22 December 1868: PRO, FO 425/91.
30 See Bonar's dispatches of 18 and 21 December 1868 with enclosures, and Apponyi's note to Clarendon of 26 December 1868 with enclosures: ibid.
31 The difference of classification renders an exact comparison impossible; but a memorandum drawn up by Louis Mallet on 8 January 1869 (PRO, FO 425/92) offers an approximate comparison of the proposed Austrian duties on cottons and woollens and the tariff of the German Customs Union.
32 Bloomfield's dispatch of 26 December 1868: PRO, FO 425/91.

the committee insisted that the lower duties should not come into effect at once, but only on 1 January 1870.[33]

Yet neither side had spoken its last word. A careful reading of Clarendon's recent dispatch to Bloomfield convinced Beust that the British government would not turn a deaf ear to a fresh proposal; and he embraced this opportunity for a last-minute understanding all the more eagerly since he could not doubt that a rejection of the supplementary convention by the *Reichsrat* would compel the British Cabinet to give the House of Commons explanations which could only create adverse publicity for Austria. Realizing that Britain would have to be offered an acceptable equivalent substitute for the *ad valorem* options of the supplementary convention, the Chancellor prevailed upon Herr von Plener, the Austrian Minister of Commerce, to make an attempt to persuade the Finance Committee to agree to a more substantial reduction of the duties by weight on cotton and woollen goods.[34]

When Plener's efforts – probably half-hearted at best – proved unavailing Beust decided to take the matter out of the hands of the Finance Committee. Instead he obtained the grudging assent of the Austrian Council of Ministers to certain reductions of the duties on cottons and woollens which, if accepted by the British government, they pledged themselves to submit promptly to the *Reichsrat*, where, Beust assured Lord Bloomfield, a majority in favour of this solution could be secured.[35]

The tariff concessions which Beust was now offering as a substitute for the *ad valorem* clause, while more generous than those suggested by the Finance Committee of the *Reichsrat,* did not

33 Instruction for Bloomfield of 19 January 1869: PRO, FO 425/92. See also Clarendon's note to Count Apponyi of the same date: HHStA, Administrative Registratur, F34, Sonderreihe, Karton 32, r2, 1 Varia, 3. Teil.
34 Beust's note to Bloomfield of 1 February 1869 (trans.), enclosed in the latter's dispatch of 2 February 1869: PRO, FO 425/92. See also Beust's notes to Ignaz von Plener of 24 January and 6 February 1869 (drafts): HHStA, Administrative Registratur, F34, Sonderreihe, Karton 32, r2, 1 Varia, 3. Teil.
35 Beust's note to Bloomfield of 19 February 1869 (trans.), enclosed in the latter's dispatch of 20 February 1869: PRO, FO 425/92, no. 21. See also Count Taaffe's note to Beust of 17 February 1869: HHStA, Administrative Registratur, F34, Sonderreihe, Karton 32, r2, 1 Varia, 3. Teil.

fully meet the British demand for a reduction of the duties on cotton and woollen goods to the level of the *Zollverein*; but they came fairly close to it. A tabular synopsis of the proposed new rates which Bloomfield forwarded to Lord Clarendon[36] showed that some articles would remain in a slightly higher, whilst others would fall into a somewhat lower, position than those in which they were placed in the tariff of the German Customs Union.

Upon receipt of Bloomfield's report, which left no doubt that the Ambassador favoured acceptance of Beust's offer, the Foreign Office consulted the Board of Trade about its merits. The opinion of the Trade Lords was embodied in a memorandum drawn up by Mallet (now Sir Louis)[37]: the Board recommended agreement to the Austrian proposals, subject to certain modifications of the tariff structure in the case of woollens. Mallet insisted that Vienna had every reason to be satisfied with this counter-proposal, all the more so since 'the withdrawal of all further claims in respect of manufactured iron in its different divisions and of many descriptions of metal wares will remain as an abatement of the treaty claims of Her Majesty's government, and ought to be considered and accepted by the government of Austria as an evidence of their wish to make every possible allowance for their political and parliamentary difficulties.'[38] But when Bloomfield informed Beust that Whitehall, while satisfied with the Austrian offer as regards cottons, insisted on further reductions of the duty on certain woollen fabrics,[39] the Chancellor replied that this was a demand Vienna could not comply with, 'for compliance with this demand would only renew that agitation in industrial circles which has been appeased with so much difficulty ... The consent of the *Reichsrat*, moreover, could not be expected.'[40]

By that time the differences between London and Vienna had

36 Enclosed in Bloomfield's dispatch of 20 February 1869: PRO, FO 425/92.
37 Sir Louis Mallet to Otway, 25 February 1869: ibid.
38 Ibid.
39 Bloomfield's note to Beust of 6 March 1869, copy enclosed in the former's dispatch of 8 March 1869: ibid.
40 Beust's note to Bloomfield of 16 March 1869 (trans.), enclosed in the latter's dispatch of 17 March 1869: PRO, FO 425/93.

boiled down to questions of technical details – e.g., whether, as the Austrians maintained but the British denied, all velvets and velvet-like webs belonged to the class of unfulled goods.[41] Disagreement on a question of timing – whether a concerted reduction of the Austrian duty on fulled cloths and hosiery from 18 to 15 florins per cwt should come into effect on 1 January 1871 (as proposed by London) or a year later – was resolved when Britain consented to the postponement on condition that the supplementary convention as amended be submitted to the *Reichsrat* for acceptance during the current session.[42]

But this latest proof of London's complaisance merely encouraged the Austrian Protectionists to insist on yet another concession. The Finance Committee of the *Reichsrat,* while accepting the proposed reduction of the tariff on cottons and woollens, refused to agree to a lowering of the duty on hosiery, which, they maintained, 'would mainly benefit Saxony not England, and utterly ruin Austrian manufacturers.'[43] When Clarendon was confronted with this latest demonstration of Vienna's stubbornness his patience snapped momentarily. He directed Bloomfield by wire to inform the Austrian government that their proposal was not acceptable.[44] However within four days the Foreign Secretary reversed his stand. On 4 May he addressed a note to Count Apponyi acquainting him 'that Her Majesty's government have given a further proof of [their] friendly spirit by informing Her Majesty's Ambassador at Vienna by telegraph this day that they consent to abandon that portion of their late proposals which applies to "hosiery," on the distinct understanding, however, that those proposals, with this exception alone, are accepted by the

41 See the document referred to in n. 40 and Bloomfield's dispatch of 13 April 1869 with enclosure: ibid.
42 See Bloomfield's telegraphic dispatch of 22 April and Clarendon's telegraphic instruction of 23 April 1869: ibid.
43 Bloomfield's telegraphic dispatch of 30 April 1869: ibid. See also Beust's instruction for Apponyi of 30 April 1869 (trans.), enclosed in Bloomfield's dispatch of 2 May 1869, and Apponyi's note to Clarendon of 3 May 1869: ibid.
44 Clarendon's telegraphic instruction of 30 April 1869: ibid.

Reichsrat during the present session of that body.'[45] Whether
Lord Clarendon had let himself be swayed by Count Apponyi,
who urgently pleaded with him for a favourable decision,[46] or
whether he was overruled in the Cabinet, a majority of which
may have wished to bring the tiresome business to an end by
making one more concession, cannot be determined.

Having obtained London's consent to the excision of the clause
referring to hosiery from the text of the supplementary convention
that was to replace the one signed by Beust on 1 July 1868 (see
above, p. 111), the Austrian government now had to fulfil their
part of the bargain and get their legislature to approve in principle
the stipulations of the revised treaty. Since the session of the
Reichsrat was drawing to a close they had to move swiftly. In
fact, a resolution rejecting the supplementary convention
of 1 July 1868, but empowering the Imperial government to substitute for it a new commercial treaty embodying the agreement
just reached with Britain, was submitted to the Lower House
by its Finance Committee as early as 7 May. Introduced by Dr
Skene, one of the most prominent champions of the manufacturing
interests in Austria, and supported by Ignaz von Plener, the Minister of Commerce, in a brief speech clearly intended to allay any
lingering suspicions of the Protectionists, the bill was carried
through the House without debate and without opposition.[47]

But no sooner had this major hurdle been cleared when a fresh
dispute between London and Vienna once more threatened to
lead to a stalemate. The issue, a highly technical one, had already
caused disagreement earlier in the year. The Austrians had
insisted, and the British denied, that all velvets and velvet-like
webs should be classified for customs purposes as unfulled goods,

---

45 Clarendon's note to Apponyi of 4 May 1869: ibid. See also Clarendon's telegraphic instruction for Bloomfield of the same date: ibid.
46 See Apponyi's note to Clarendon of 3 May 1869: ibid.
47 See the minutes of the *Haus der Abgeordneten*, 1868–9, pp. 6027ff. and 6051ff.
   See also Bloomfield's dispatches of 7 and 10 May 1869 with enclosures: PRO,
   FO 425/93.

which, when imported into Austria, were charged with a much higher duty than fulled wares.[48] But a few weeks later Vienna unexpectedly had seemed to give in. On 18 May 1869 Beust, having learned from the Minister of Commerce that the Austrian customs officers had, as early as March 1868, received instructions to follow the practice of the *Zollverein* and treat the textiles in question as fulled wares,[49] informed Lord Bloomfield of this fact.[50]

Thus for all practical purposes the question had appeared to be settled in accordance with British wishes. However the Lords of Trade, whom the Foreign Office asked for an opinion, declared themselves entirely dissatisfied with this informal solution. The issue of an instruction to the Imperial custom-houses, they insisted, was no substitute for a stipulation recorded in the treaty – all the less so since, as they had discovered, the tariff schedule which the Austrian government proposed to annex to the new supplementary convention still listed woollen velvets among unfulled fabrics.[51] Clarendon fully concurred with these views of the Board of Trade and instructed Bloomfield accordingly.[52] The British resolve not to rely on a mere custom-house instruction to secure admission into Austria of British velvets under the category of fulled wares was strengthened by information reaching London according to which the Austrian customs officers had never acted upon those instructions.[53]

The Austrians on their part flatly refused the British demand to have that tariff modification recorded in conventional form. All they promised was that their Minister of Commerce would 'listen to complaints and cause redress to be given' if, contrary to expectation, any custom-house should fail to act in the sense

---

48 See Bloomfield's note to Beust of 6 March, Beust's note to Bloomfield of 16 March (trans.), enclosed in the latter's dispatch of 17 March 1869, and Clarendon's instruction for Bloomfield of 6 April 1869 with enclosure: ibid.
49 See Plener's note to Beust of 11 May 1869: HHStA, Administrative Registratur, F34, Sonderreihe, Karton 32, r2, 1 Varia, 3. Teil.
50 Beust's note to Bloomfield of 18 May 1869: PRO, FO 425/93.
51 Sir Louis Mallet's note to Mr Otway of 31 May 1869: ibid.
52 Clarendon's instruction for Bloomfield of 1 June 1869: ibid.
53 See the copy of Bloomfield's note to Beust of 2 June 1868, enclosed in his dispatch to Clarendon of the same date; ibid.

of the above-mentioned guidelines.[54] The reason given for their negative answer was the usual one: compliance with the British claim, Beust declared, might expose the Imperial government to a parliamentary defeat.[55] 'This may be true,' was Bloomfield's comment; 'for the government majority in the Lower House of the Reichsrat is mainly dependent on industrial monopolists.'[56]

At this juncture, when a breakdown of the negotiation seemed once more imminent, Beust, with the consent of the Minister of Commerce, produced another conciliatory offer.[57] It was designed to allay British suspicions while avoiding a fresh confrontation of the Austrian government with their legislature. Based on a scheme which a few weeks earlier had been urged on Beust by Baron Max von Gagern, the head of the commercial section of his Ministry,[58] but which at that time had been rejected by Ignaz von Plener,[59] the proposal envisaged the addition to the supplementary convention of a Final Protocol and an explanatory note supposed fully to clarify the issue of the velvet-like woollens.

As it turned out the wording of these appendices as drafted by the Austrians, so far from removing any ambiguity, would only have created further uncertainties. Thus the Board of Trade, after conferring with representatives of the woollen trade practically conversant with the technical questions involved, came to the conclusion that the government should not, under any circumstances, become a party to the arrangement proposed by Beust. 'The definitions and distinctions [of the draft Protocol],' the Trade Lords declared, 'are of a nature so capricious, and often so unintelligible that it would be most undesirable on every account to recognize them by an international engagement.'[60] They ques-

---

54 See Beust's note to Bloomfield (trans.) of 9 July, enclosed in the latter's dispatch of 10 July 1869: ibid.
55 Ibid.
56 Bloomfield's dispatch of 19 July 1869: ibid.
57 Beust's note to Bloomfield (trans.) of 9 August, enclosed in the latter's dispatch of 10 August 1869: ibid.
58 Gagern's memorandum of 28 June 1869: HHStA, Administrative Registratur, F34, Sonderreihe, Karton 32, r2, 1 Varia, 4. Teil.
59 Plener's note to Beust of 6 July 1869: ibid.
60 Sir Louis Mallet's note to Spring Rice of 17 September 1869: PRO, FO 425/93.

tioned, moreover, whether the Protocol, if signed, would be more acceptable to the *Reichsrat* than the tariff modification which, as Beust maintained, the Austrian government could scarcely propose to the legislature without losing its confidence.

On this latter point, which Bloomfield had been instructed to raise with the Austrians,[61] Beust was able to reassure the Ambassador. He pointed out that the stipulations contained in his draft of the Protocol did not require the sanction of the *Reichsrat*, since, having been cited in the Final Protocol to Austria's treaty with the *Zollverein* of 9 March 1868, they already formed the subject of an international agreement.[62]

Beust's admission that the regulations concerning the classification of velvet-like textures, which he offered to record in a Protocol, had already been embodied in an international instrument was received with great interest in London. For, as the Board of Trade pointed out, 'if such an instrument [was] already in force between Austria and Prussia, British trade [was] already equally entitled to claim any advantages which may be derived from it, under the most-favoured-nation article of the treaty of 1865.'[63] Having ascertained that the Final Protocol annexed to Austria's treaty with the *Zollverein* actually contained the regulations in question, Clarendon directed the British Chargé d'Affaires in Vienna to obtain Beust's formal acknowledgement of the British claim to equal treatment under the most-favoured-nation clause of the Anglo-Austrian treaty of 16 December 1865.[64]

Assuming that this demand would be met – and a refusal was hardly to be imagined – Britain could not expect to gain any further concessions beyond those which she had already secured in previous negotiations or which had become due to her in consequence of the most-favoured-nation clause of the December treaty. Therefore, acting upon advice received earlier from the Board of Trade,[65] the Foreign Secretary let it be known in Vienna

61 Instruction for Bloomfield of 22 September 1869: ibid.
62 Beust's note to Bloomfield (trans.) of 13 October, enclosed in the latter's dispatch of 14 October 1869: ibid.
63 Sir Louis Mallet's note to Mr Otway of 3 November 1869: ibid.
64 Instruction for R. Lytton-Bulwer of 22 November 1869: ibid.
65 Sir Louis Mallet's note to Mr Otway of 3 November 1869: ibid.

that the British government were no longer interested in the supplementary convention which Article v of the treaty of 1865 had stipulated. 'It appears to Her Majesty's government,' he informed R. Lytton-Bulwer, the Chargé d'Affaires,

that all the objects in view can be obtained by means of a convention between the two governments, the preamble of which should state that the assent of the *Reichsrat* not having been obtained for the convention of 1868, the two governments have agreed to the following conditions:

1. On the side of Austria, the reduction of duties on cottons and woollens approved by the Finance Committee; and the confirmation to England of the tariff of duties annexed to the Austro-Zollverein treaty of 1868.
2. On the side of England, the withdrawal of claims under the articles of the treaty of 1865 and of the Final Protocol which have practically been found incapable of execution.[66]

This short convention[67] which Lytton-Bulwer was instructed to propose, more specifically the provision referring to the abatement of the duties on British cottons and woollens, was consistent with the resolution adopted by the *Reichsrat* on 7 May 1869 (see above, p. 125); its approval by that legislative body therefore could hardly be withheld. Beyond that the proposed text merely recorded advantages already conceded to Britain under the treaty of 1865. It would have been an exhibition of more than ordinary perversity had the Austrians found fault with the proposal. As a matter of fact, Count Beust, when presented with it, at once assured the British Chargé d'Affaires that he anticipated a 'speedy and satisfactory termination of these long protracted negotiations on the basis now proposed by [Clarendon].'[68] On this occasion not even the Minister of Commerce raised any objections,[69] and things began to move quickly. Indeed it now was the Austrians

66 Instruction for R. Lytton-Bulwer of 22 November 1869: ibid.
67 See the draft enclosed in Sir Louis Mallet's note to Mr Otway of 18 November, and transmitted to Lytton-Bulwer by Clarendon on 22 November 1869: ibid.
68 Lytton-Bulwer's dispatch of 9 December 1869: ibid.
69 See Plener's note to Beust of 13 December 1869: HHStA, Administrative Registratur, F34, Sonderreihe, Karton 32, r2, 1 Varia, 2. Teil (misplaced).

who urged dispatch: they insisted that the treaty must be signed before the end of the year.[70] So anxious was Beust to speed up the proceedings that he declared himself willing to sign with Lytton-Bulwer without waiting for the arrival of the latter's full powers.[71] But Lord Bloomfield, who had been on leave of absence, left London in the evening of 25 December,[72] and reached Vienna in time to affix his seal and signature to the document. The ceremony took place at the Imperial Chancellery of State at twelve o'clock on 30 December 1869.[73] Having obtained the Imperial sanction on 3 January 1870,[74] the convention was submitted to the Lower and Upper Houses of Austria and Hungary, whose approval was given early in February.[75] The ratifications were exchanged on 23 February.[76]

Remembering the reams and reams of reports he had sent to London over a period of nine years and the untold hours he had spent perusing his instructions or arguing with Austrian statesmen about some contentious clause in yet another draft of a commercial convention or protocol, Lord Bloomfield may well have asked himself whether the game had been worth the candle. Could it not have been foreseen from the very start that, in the words of Horace,

Parturiunt montes, nascetur ridiculus mus?

Such doubt, though natural, would not, however, have been entirely justified. Admittedly the hopes created in London in 1862 by a decision of the Austrian Council of Ministers to revise their country's protectionist policy had not been fulfilled: a British offer

70 Lytton-Bulwer's telegraphic dispatch of 21 December 1869: PRO, FO 425/93.
71 Ibid.
72 Clarendon's telegram to Lytton-Bulwer of 22 December 1869: ibid.
73 Bloomfield's dispatch of 30 December 1869: ibid.
74 HHStA, Administrative Registratur, F34, Sonderreihe, Karton 32, r2, 1 Varia, 4. Teil.
75 Bloomfield's telegraphic dispatches of 7 and 12 February 1870: PRO, FO 425/93.
76 Bloomfield's telegraphic dispatch of 23 February 1870: ibid.

to negotiate a commercial convention on the model of the Cobden treaty or the recently concluded Franco-Prussian treaty of commerce had been rejected. The failure of the missionary efforts of the British Chambers of Commerce and the successful tactics of Austrian businessmen and bureaucrats in bringing to nought the Joint Commission of Inquiry in the spring of 1865 should have served as further warnings that the Protectionists would put up a fierce resistance to any major move in the direction of Free Trade.

But the exigencies of Austria's public finance strengthened the hands of Count Mensdorff, the Minister of Foreign Affairs, who, on political grounds, seems to have been very much in favour of treating with Britain. Though his promise to conclude a liberal treaty of commerce was contained only in a personal letter of his to Somerset Beaumont, the representative of British bankers, and though the British loan which that promise was intended to facilitate did not materialize, formal negotiations were started on 1 November, and after a few weeks' bickering led to the signature, on 16 December 1865, of a commercial convention. However the satisfaction of the British negotiators and their government at the results proved premature. For the December treaty and the Final Protocol annexed to it contained a number of highly ambiguous stipulations which, as has been shown, gave rise to long and acrimonious disputes, and, 'having practically been found incapable of execution,'[77] were in the end suppressed under Article III of the treaty signed on 30 December 1869.

Yet it would be wrong to write off the treaty of 1865 as wholly nugatory from a British point of view. Its second article, which came into force on 1 January 1867, placed British subjects and commerce within the dominions of the Emperor 'in every respect upon the footing of the most favoured nation'; they were to 'share in all the advantages and favours which are enjoyed by the commerce and subjects of any third Power.'[78] By virtue of this article British imports into Austria came to enjoy the same reductions of duties which the Empire granted to the French under the treaty

77 Instruction for Lytton-Bulwer of 22 November 1869: ibid.
78 *British and Foreign State Papers* (1864–5), LV, 8.

of 11 November 1866 and to the German Customs Union under the treaty of 9 March 1868.

Nor was the treaty concluded on 30 December 1869 wholly without value to the British. To be sure, it finally released the Austrian government from heavy obligations which they had assumed under Article III of the earlier convention – but which they had never carried out – namely to reduce their import duties on British goods to 25 per cent of the value after 1 January 1867 and to 20 per cent after 1 January 1870.[79] Yet Britain had not yielded on these points without receiving some compensation in the form of reduced duties on cottons and woollens. All in all, the British had not done too badly in their dealings with Austria, considering that they had little to offer in the way of reciprocity: for by their unilateral moves towards Free Trade they had given away most of their bargaining counters before the start of the negotiations. This was admitted by Gladstone the day before the convention with Austria was tabled in the House of Commons. 'It is unquestionably true,' the Prime Minister said in reply to a question by Somerset Beaumont, 'that the margin which remains open to us for any commercial treaty is very narrow.'[80]

This being the case, the enthusiasm for commercial conventions which the Cobden Treaty had engendered in Britain was on the wane, at any rate in certain government circles. Mr Lowe, the Chancellor of the Exchequer, when urged by a deputation of the Associated Chambers of Commerce to negotiate commercial treaties with Spain and Portugal, roundly declared 'that he was not in favour of treaties of commerce; he was not in favour of their negotiation ... If [the government] were to negotiate with Spain and Portugal they would in effect be conferring an immense advantage upon them for their illiberality.'[81]

The open or insidious resistance which the British had encountered all along in their recent negotiations with the Austro-

79 Ibid., pp. 8f.
80 *Parliamentary Debates* (Hansard), 3rd s., vol. CXCIX, col. 883 (Commons, 28 February 1870).
81 *The Times* (London), 25 February 1870, p. 3.

Hungarian Empire taught them yet another unpalatable truth, which Sir Louis Mallet stated succinctly in these words: 'The progress of representative institutions in Europe, with all their admitted advantages, has, for a time at least, been accompanied with the drawback of giving renewed expression to the Protectionist feelings which still exist so generally in the industrial classes in the Continental countries.'[82]

Except for his qualifying clause ('for a time at least') Mallet's melancholy diagnosis was fully confirmed by developments in the following decades, when the continental nations of Europe one by one revised their tariffs in the direction of Protectionism. That revival, in the last quarter of the nineteenth century, of economic nationalism must have appeared to many Austrians a vindication of their country's earlier resistance to British persuasion and pressure. Ernst von Plener undoubtedly could count on the sympathy of a majority of his readers when, in his memoirs, he bestowed high praise on his father for his skill and determination in thwarting Britain's efforts to drag Austria into the Free Trade camp.[83]

82 Mallet's memorandum of 3 November 1869: PRO, FO 425/93.
83 See Ernst von Plener, *Erinnerungen* (Stuttgart & Leipzig, 1911), I, 180–3 and 210–11.

Bibliography

PRIMARY SOURCES

I *Manuscript sources*

Public Record Office, London (PRO)

FO 7/586–9, 592, 593, 595, 598, 599, 605–8, 611–14, 625, 626, 629–36, 638, 640, 648, 649, 652–4, 656, 664, 665, 667, 669–74, 681, 682, 685–95, 701, 703–6, 711, 715–17, 719
FO 97/72
30/22/43; 30/22/45

Haus-, Hof- und Staatsarchiv, Vienna (HHStA)

Politisches Archiv VIII, England, Kartons 53, 54, 57–9, 64, 66
Administrative Registratur des Ministeriums des Äussern, F34: Handel, Grossbritannien, Karton 5; Sonderreihe, Karton 41; Sonderreihe, Karton 32, r2, 1 Varia; Kabinettsarchiv, Ministerratsprotokolle, 1860–5

Finanz- und Hofkammerarchiv, Vienna (FHKA)

Finanzarchiv, Präsidium des Finanzministeriums, 1860

Allgemeines Verwaltungsarchiv, Vienna (AVA)

Präsidium des Handelsministeriums, 1865

British Museum, Add. Mss 44183 (Gladstone Papers), ff. 403–408v

Bodleian Library, Ms Clarendon, Dep. C. 91, ff. 187–202

II *Printed sources*

Correspondence respecting Commercial Negotiations with Austria, PRO, FO 425/78–80

Correspondence with Her Majesty's Chargé d'Affaires at Vienna regarding the Resumption of the Sittings of the Mixed Commission, PRO, FO 425/88

Further Correspondence respecting the Resumption of the Sittings of the Anglo-Austrian Mixed Commission, PRO, FO 425/89

Correspondence respecting the Proceedings of the Anglo-Austrian Tariff Commission, PRO, FO 425/90–1, 93

Further Correspondence respecting the Proceedings of the Anglo-Austrian Tariff Commission, PRO, FO 425/92

WEMYSS, ROSSLYN [i.e., VICTORIA WEMYSS, BARONESS WESTER-WEMYSS]. *Memoirs and Letters of the Right Hon. Sir Robert Morier, G.C.B.* 2 vols. London, 1911

GLADSTONE, W.E., *The Financial Statements of 1853 and 1860 to 1865.* London, 1865

Parliamentary Debates (Hansard), 3rd s., vols. CLXVIII, CXCII, CXCIII, CXCIX

British and Foreign State Papers, Vols. L (1859–60), LV (1864–5), LVIII (1867–8)

The Times (London), 29 October 1862, 25 October 1864, 23 November 1865, 25 February 1870

The Northern Daily Express, 4 November 1862

AN ENGLISHMAN [BARON HENRY DE WORMS]. *The Austro-Hungarian Empire and the Policy of Count Beust.* London, 1870

BEUST, FRIEDRICH FERDINAND COUNT VON. *Memoirs.* 2 vols. 2nd ed. London, 1887

MALLET, SIR LOUIS. *Reciprocity: a Letter to Mr. Thomas Bayley Potter, M.P.* Printed for the Cobden Club. London, Paris & New York, [1879]

[AUSTRIA]. *Stenographische Protokolle, Reichsrat, Haus der Abgeordneten.* 1868–9

Austria. Wochenschrift für Volkswirthschaft und Statistik, vol. XVI, no. 47 (21 November 1864)

Der Volkswirth. Wochenblatt für den Geld-, Effecten- und Waarenverkehr, vol. VII, no. 45 (11 November 1864)

WORKS CITED

I *Books*

Allgemeine deutsche Biographie, vol. LV
BEER, ADOLF. *Die Finanzen Oesterreichs im XIX. Jahrhundert.* Prague, 1877
BEER, ADOLF. *Die österreichische Handelspolitik im neunzehnten Jahrhundert.* Vienna, 1891
BELL, HERBERT C.F. *Lord Palmerston,* vol. II. London, 1936
CLAPHAM, SIR JOHN. *An Economic History of Modern Britain,* vol. II. Cambridge, 1932
COLEMAN, D.C. *The British Paper Industry 1495–1860.* Oxford, 1958
DUNHAM, ARTHUR L. *The Anglo-French Treaty of Commerce of 1860.* Ann Arbor, 1930
Encyclopedia of the Social Sciences, vol. XIV
GILLE, BERTRAND. *Histoire de la maison Rothschild,* vol. II. Geneva, 1967
Handwörterbuch der Sozialwissenschaften, vol. X
NORTHCOTE, SIR STAFFORD H. *Twenty Years of Financial Policy.* London, 1862
Österreichisches biographisches Lexikon, vols. I and II
Dictionary of Political Economy, ed. R.H. Inglis Palgrave, Vol. III
PLENER, ERNST VON. *Erinnerungen,* vol. I. Stuttgart & Leipzig, 1911
STEIN, LORENZ. *Geschichte der socialen Bewegung in Frankreich.* Leipzig, 1850/1
STEIN, LORENZ. *Lehrbuch der Volkswirthschaft.* Vienna, 1858
WEINZIERL-FISCHER, ERIKA. *Die österreichischen Kondordate von 1855 und 1933.* Vienna, 1960
WURZBACH, CONSTANT VON. *Biographisches Lexikon des Kaiserthums Österreich,* vol. XLIV. Vienna, 1883

II *Articles*

STEEFEL, LAWRENCE B. 'The Rothschilds and the Austrian Loan of 1865,' *The Journal of Modern History,* vol. VIII (1936)

WERNER, KARL HEINZ. 'Österreichs Industrie- und Aussenhandelspolitik 1848 bis 1948,' in Hans Mayer, ed., *Hundert Jahre österreichischer Wirtschaftsentwicklung.* Vienna, 1949

Index

Certain references, especially to persons whose letters and dispatches have been our chief source of information (such as Lord Bloomfield, A.G.G. Bonar, Sir Robert Morier, Sir Louis Mallet, Count Apponyi, Count Rechberg, Baron Beust, and others) are selective. To have given exhaustive listings of such names would have served no useful purpose. The names of authors listed in our bibliography are not generally included in the index.

the Board of Trade, 5, 44; as member of the Commission of Inquiry, 44ff; received in private audience by Francis Joseph, 46f; expresses his dissatisfaction to Kalchberg and Mensdorff with the lack of progress of the Commission of Inquiry, 48f, 60; returns to London in disappointment, 50f; optimistic about the assumption of office of Belcredi's Cabinet, 62f

India-rubber wares, Austrian duties on, 96
Iron duties, Austrian, 90, 93, 123
Italy: war between Austria and (1866), concluded by the peace treaty of Vienna, 83; commercial negotiations of with Austria (1867), 85. *See also* Piedmont

Jablonowski, Prince Karl, Member of the Austrian Upper Chamber, Vice-President of the Carl-Ludwigs Railway, Vice-President of the Commission of Inquiry, 49
Joint Commissions. *See* Commission of Inquiry; Mixed Commission
Jute, Austrian import duties on, 65, 76

Kalchberg, Baron Josef, Austrian Acting Minister of Commerce, 35, 41, 58; selects the Austrian members of the Commission of Inquiry and serves as its chairman, 42; interviews Hutt and Morier, 46; interested in obtaining British capital for Austrian railway construction, 46; secures a strong representation of Protectionists on the Commission of Inquiry, 47; assures the Tariff Committee of the *Reichsrat* that the revised tariff will not soon be altered, 47, 59, 62; agrees to a reconstruction of the Commission of Inquiry, 49f; criticizes Hock's suggestion to start commercial negotiations with France, 54
Kalchegger von Kalchberg. *See* Kalchberg
Kaschau iron works, 90
Königgrätz, battle of. *See* Sadowa

Larisch, Count Johann, Austrian Minister of Finance: authorizes Beaumont to make the terms of the Austrian loan known to English capitalists, 64; instructs Becke to break off the negotiations with Baron James Rothschild, 73
Larisch-Mönnich. *See* Larisch
Liebmann, Max, of Huddersfield, delegate sent to Vienna by the British Chambers of Commerce, 30